Walking
Ayrshire, Renfrewshire and L

Clan Walk Guides

Walking Ayrshire, Renfrewshire and Lanarkshire

Walking Scotland Series
Volume 20

Mary Welsh
and
Christine Isherwood

First published by Clan Books, 2012

ISBN 978 1 873597 36 1

Clan Books
Clandon House
The Cross, Doune
Perthshire
FK16 6BE

Printed and bound in Great Britain by
Bell & Bain Ltd., Glasgow

Publisher's Note

With the publication of this volume and its companion "Walking Fife, The Ochils, Tayside and the Forth Valley", the authors and publishers are celebrating the completion of the "*Walking Scotland Series*." Each of the twenty-one volumes in the series aspires to offer for all those who walk for pleasure a balanced cross-section of expeditions ranging from leisurely strolls to challenging mountain ridges and summits.

This new volume is typical in that it succeeds in finding and describing just such an exciting cocktail of outings in counties too often denigrated as a post-industrial desert. Try it and you will discover that there is plenty of beauty and fascinating history here to be enjoyed.

Our task is not entirely complete. Over the coming years we intend to re-visit the walks described in each volume as it falls due for re-printing. Walking Scotland Series has gained an appreciative following for its comprehensive and wide-ranging depiction of the Scottish countryside, and it will continue to be up-to-date and relevant.

The Authors' Golden Rules for Good, Safe Walking

- Wear suitable clothes and take adequate waterproofs.
- Walk in strong footwear; walking boots are advisable.
- Carry the relevant map and a compass and know how to use them.
- Carry a whistle; remember six long blasts repeated at one minute intervals is the distress signal.
- Do not walk alone, and tell someone where you are going.
- If mist descends, return.
- Keep all dogs under strict control. Observe all "No Dogs" notices – they are there for very good reasons.

Contents

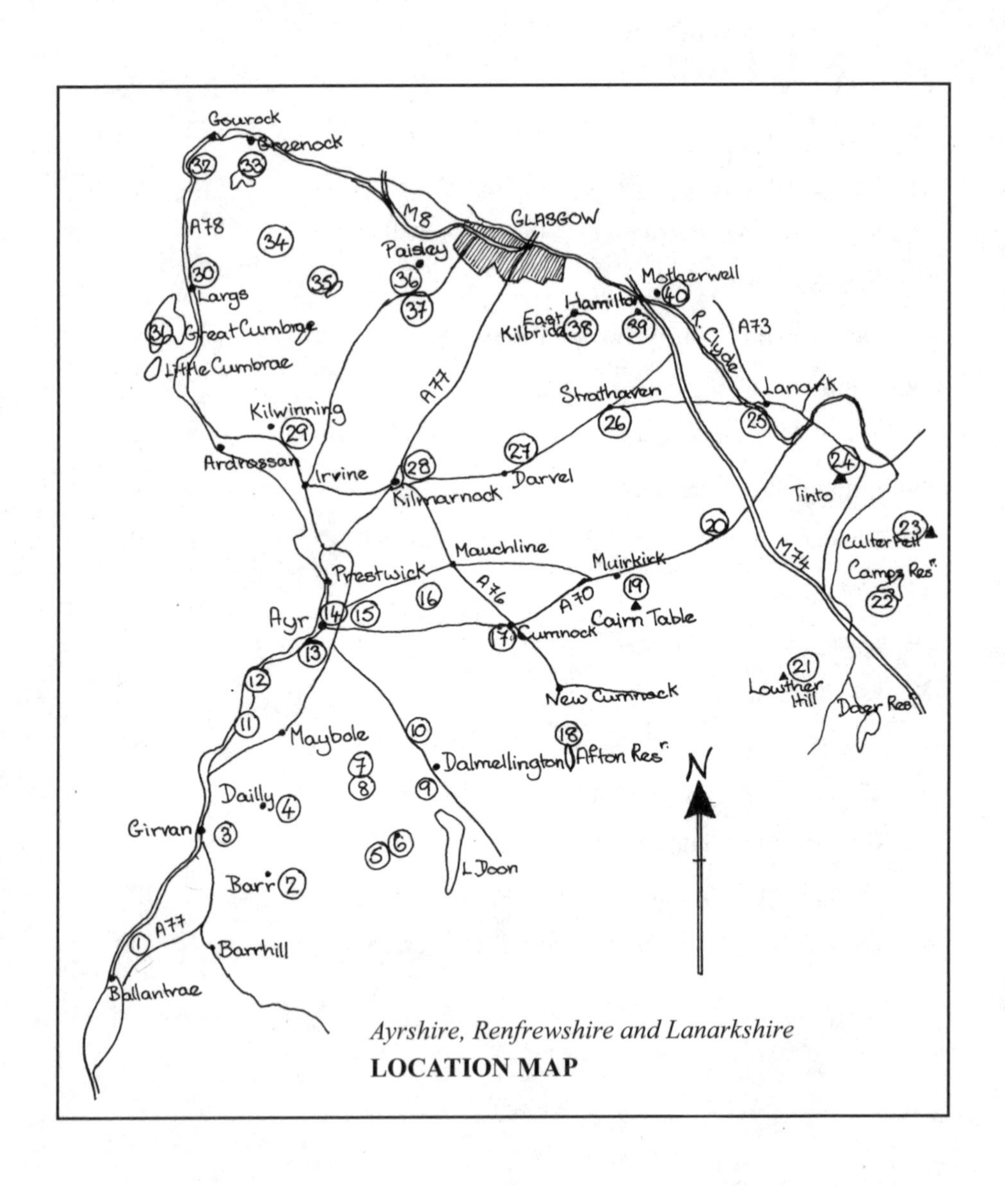

Ayrshire, Renfrewshire and Lanarkshire

LOCATION MAP

Walk 1

Knockdolian

Park in a grassy layby, grid ref 120848, on the west side of the B7044. Opposite the layby is a sign pointing to the start of the hill climb. Access the layby by driving for 3 miles/5km along the B-road after leaving the A77 at Ballantrae.

The **valley of the River Stinchar**, one of the most beautiful in Southern Scotland, lies in Carrick, South Ayrshire. Rising in the Galloway Forest, the river flows through the villages of Barr, Pinwherry and Colmonell, reaching the sea at Ballantrae. The distinctive hill of Knockdolian, an ancient volcanic plug, rises at the lower end of the valley and is a landmark for miles around.

1 From the parking layby, climb the short steep bank to a gate in the hedge. Beyond, bear left and slant upwards across the huge field to a gate

Knockdolian

in the wall or, if there is a crop growing, curve left round the edge of the pasture. Continue on the path beyond, which climbs steadily and easily. It winds round on the south side of the hill, above the Stinchar Valley, but then becomes obscure. Ascend a shallow dip beside a broken wall. Where the wall reaches a crag there is a clear gap and the path continues round and up the hill from here. In places it divides, but the route is never really in doubt and becomes clearer as you get higher. It passes rocky outcrops that support lichen and cushions of heather. As you near the top, long ridges of rock have delightful floral gardens between them.

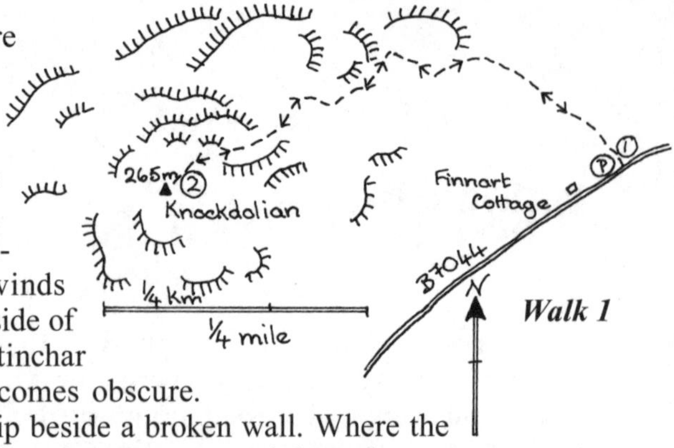

Walk 1

2 The splendid summit is reached by continuing on the narrow path. Stand by the trig point (857ft/265m) and enjoy the magnificent view. Look for Ailsa Craig, Kintyre, Holy Island and the Arran mountains. You might even spot the grey smudge of Ireland. Look into Galloway and try to name its fine mountains. Below you can see a small loch, The Dam, and then north-east the glorious Stinchar valley. North, along the curving coastline, lie Girvan, Ayr and beyond. Pause long enough and you might spot a pair of sparrowhawks performing a wonderful aerial dance. You might also be able to look down on a buzzard or a kestrel. Then return by the same pleasant route.

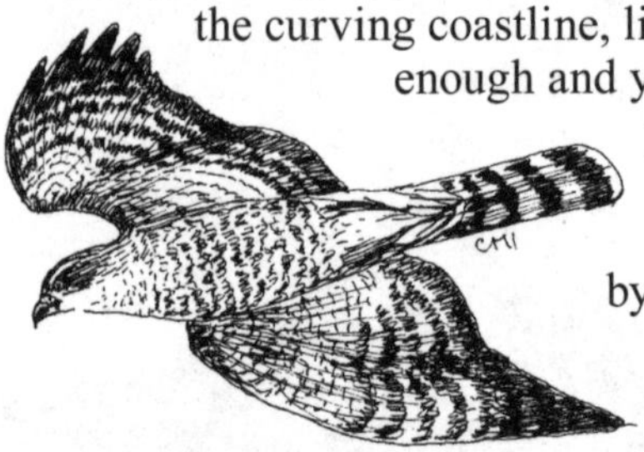

Sparrowhawk

Practicals

Type of walk: *A great climb, that shouldn't be missed, on a pleasingly graded path. Suitable for all.*

Distance: 1½ miles/2.5km

Time: 1½ hours

Maps: OS Explorer 317/Landranger 76

Walk 2

The Devil's Trail, Barr

Park in the walkers' car park, 1km east from the village of Barr, grid ref 287943. To access this, leave the B734 at Stinchar Bridge and drive through the village, keeping by the burn. After ½ mile/1km turn left uphill to the car park.

Attractive Barr is a conservation village. From it are many walking trails developed by the South Ayrshire Council and Scottish Enterprise Ayrshire.

The name of the trail originates from **a legend**. The Laird of Changue said he would sell his soul to the devil in return for great riches but then he changed his mind. A tremendous battle took place between the two and the Laird won.

During a snowstorm in January 1913, young Christopher McTaggart, known as Kirstie, set out to tend his sheep. When he hadn't returned

Barr

home by night fall, his twin brother and friends searched the moorland and found him dying of exposure. **The Cairn** stands close by where Kirstie lost his life.

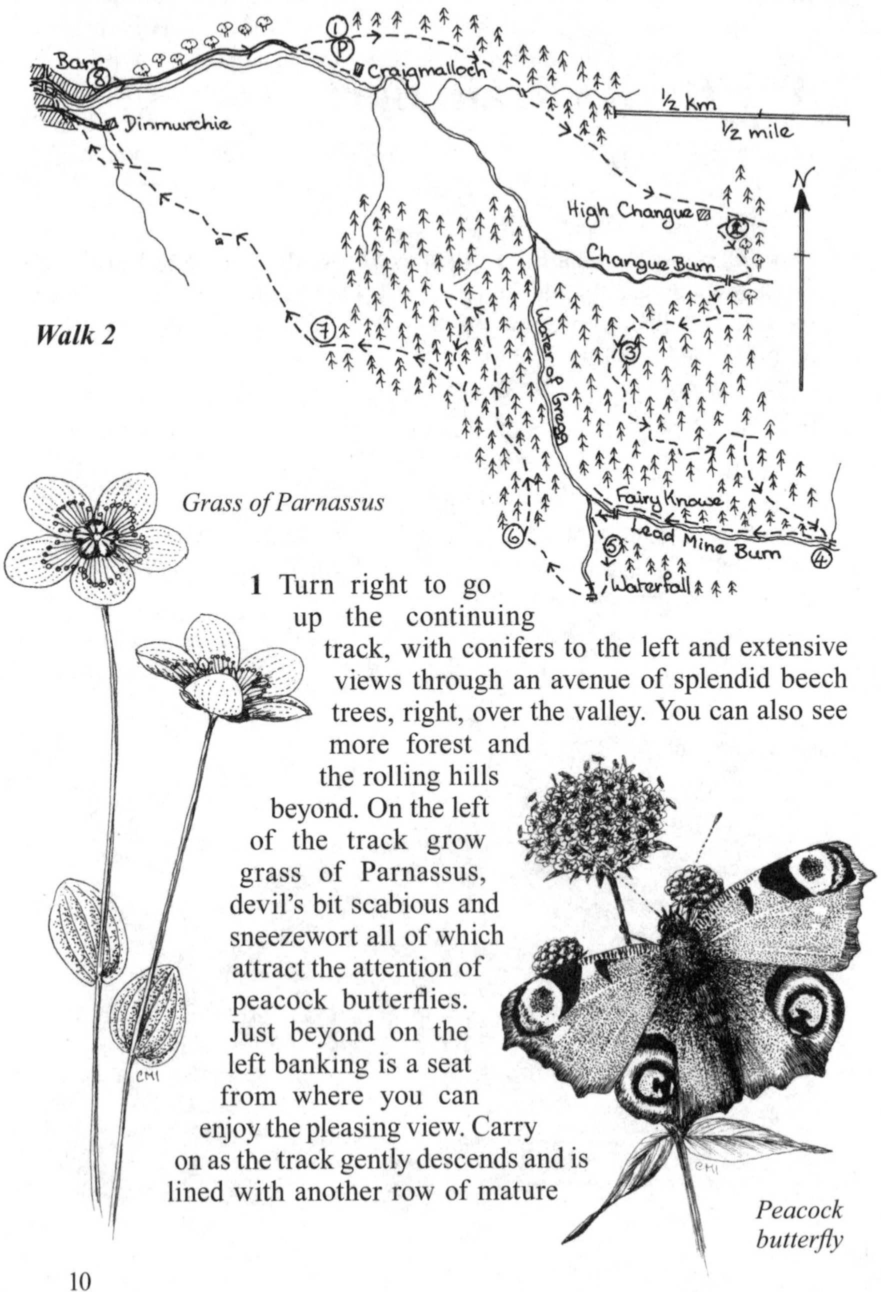

Walk 2

Grass of Parnassus

1 Turn right to go up the continuing track, with conifers to the left and extensive views through an avenue of splendid beech trees, right, over the valley. You can also see more forest and the rolling hills beyond. On the left of the track grow grass of Parnassus, devil's bit scabious and sneezewort all of which attract the attention of peacock butterflies. Just beyond on the left banking is a seat from where you can enjoy the pleasing view. Carry on as the track gently descends and is lined with another row of mature

Peacock butterfly

beech. Go round the barrier beyond High Changue farm and carry on for a few steps.

2 Look for a waymark on the left and take, opposite, a path leading down into the forest. A short way along the path moves out of the trees and winds left as a delightful grassy trod. Descend steadily with lime trees on either side. Cross a footbridge over a gurgling stream and climb steeply up the continuing path where the trees lie back and allow shrubs and flowers enough light to thrive. At the T-junction, walk right along a track pausing to look high up in the tall spruce to spot crossbills feeding on the plentiful cones.

3 Head on along this old track where you might spot a shrew crossing from one side to the other in its frantic search for insects on which it has to feed all the time to survive. The path winds on through the forest and eventually comes to a waymark on the left, directing you right along a gently descending ride. If you are walking this route in early autumn look out for the pretty russula toadstools with their magenta caps. Continue down and down until you reach a lonely valley through which flows the Lead Mine Burn. At this T-junction you might like to make a short diversion to visit the memorial to Christopher McTaggart, generally called Kirstie's cairn, if so turn left and walk the ride. Then return to the T-junction and carry on along the track.

4 As you continue along the level track, the forest rises steeply to your right and, to your left, across the burn, tower steep grassy slopes. Then the track arcs left and drops to the valley bottom. Take the path branching left. Here the Lead Mine Burn flows sweetly and a heron feeds quietly. Cross the bridge over the burn and turn right to walk along the far bank. Overhead a buzzard circles. Climb several wooden steps and wind left and before you rises the 'nose' of the steep grassy slope. Small steps, well supported with sturdy wooden risers, climb steadily up this long stretch of brae. If it seems an uncomfortable climb, keep looking at each step as you ascend and don't look down on either side.

5 At the top, walk the on-going path high above the deep ravine to your right. If you also find the path, which slopes a little towards the edge, rather disconcerting, move into the long grass on the left. The path carries on easily and away from the edge around the head of the wide gorge and descends comfortably to a footbridge. Under this a burn tumbles down a steep drop and continues to unite with the Lead Mine Burn to become the Water of Gregg. From the footbridge carry on the fine grassy path, where many grass of Parnassus flower, and wind round into the forest. Here you might spot some magnificent Fly Agaric toadstools.

6 Walk on along the ride that has masses of dog lichen growing in the grass below your boots. Follow the ride as it climbs gently to a junction of tracks. Turn sharp left and climb steadily to a waymark that directs you right. Head on the narrow path along an overgrown area where you have to weave about a little to find the driest way. Very soon you reach a V-shaped stile. Beyond, climb the next stile and then step right to climb another.

7 Now begin your descent towards the village of Barr. An overgrown path descends a long outrake, with a low wall to your left and a fence to the right. Press on down to climb the next stile. Beyond go on descending and then wind left towards a barn with a red corrugated roof. Pass in front of it and wind down with the path. Beyond the waymarked kissing gate, go on down the track, keeping to the right of a row of hawthorns to pass through the next kissing gate. Walk on to take another gate on the left and walk ahead beside a small plantation on the right. At its end, climb a waymarked stile and drop down the pasture to an awkward stile over the fence on the right. Turn left and walk on down. Head right, over grass, to cross the river on a fine iron bridge into the village, which you will enjoy exploring.

8 Walk, right, east, and follow the single track road, with a few passing places, and then turn left at the signpost for the car park.

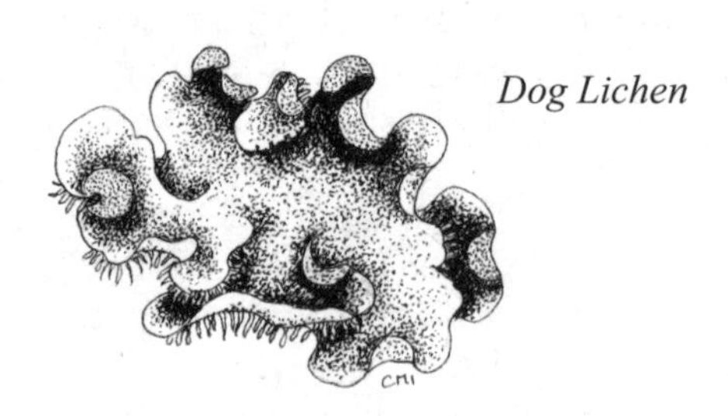

Dog Lichen

Practicals

Type of walk: *A good, mainly forest walk with lots of shelter from a gusty wind. Quite challenging in parts. Open areas and good views.*

Distance:	6½ miles/10.5km
Time:	3–4 hours
Maps:	OS Explorer 317/Landranger 76

Walk 3

Dow Hill, Girvan

Park in the Shalloch Park seashore car park, overlooking the glorious sands of the Firth of Clyde, grid ref 182964, where there are toilets and a good snack bar.

It takes only a small effort to get to the top of Dow Hill but the rewards are stunning. On a sunny day, besides sunbathing, you have wonderful views over the Firth of Clyde to Ailsa Craig, the Isle of Arran and Kintyre.You can also explore Dow Hill, the site of an ancient **hill fort**.

Dow Hill, Girvan

1 Walk back, left, along the A77. Just before the roundabout cross the A-road with care, and take the second right, signed 'Ayr Avoiding Low Bridge'. After 100yds/30m along look for the sign, on the left side of the road, directing you through a gate on the opposite side. Continue uphill on a good reinforced farm track to enter deciduous woodland. Follow the track as it leads you to a stone bridge over the Ayr to Stranraer railway line. Cross and wind on up through woodland, where the way can be muddy after rain.

2 Once out of the trees and with the slopes of Dow Hill to your right, the track becomes drier. Carry on up, now with woodland to your left,

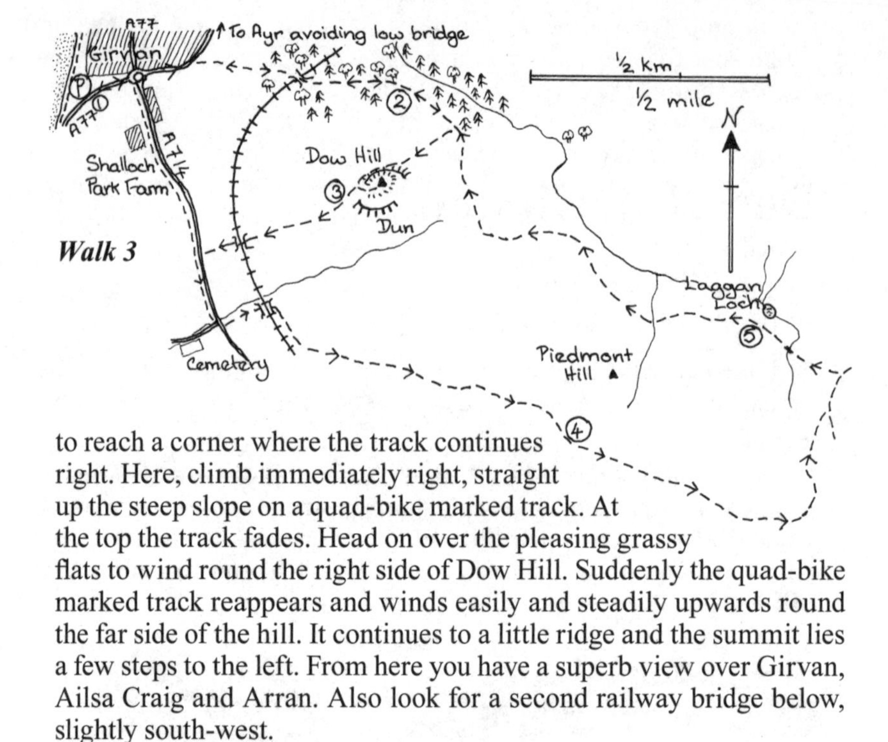

to reach a corner where the track continues right. Here, climb immediately right, straight up the steep slope on a quad-bike marked track. At the top the track fades. Head on over the pleasing grassy flats to wind round the right side of Dow Hill. Suddenly the quad-bike marked track reappears and winds easily and steadily upwards round the far side of the hill. It continues to a little ridge and the summit lies a few steps to the left. From here you have a superb view over Girvan, Ailsa Craig and Arran. Also look for a second railway bridge below, slightly south-west.

3 To return cross the fence by a stile and descend towards the tunnel under the railway bridge. Continue to a gate onto the A714. Cross with care and walk left. After 200m further on a minor road joins it on the right coming from a cemetery. Cross the A714 again here and head uphill on a track along the edge of a field. Go under the railway line, where there is a gate, and wind round to the right, then left again, still following the track up the field. Beyond the next gate the track becomes much grassier and runs through gorse up the hillside along the side of a valley. Buzzards hang in the air above and ravens swoop and tumble, and from January onwards you may hear skylarks singing. There are good views back to Byne Hill and the Grey Hills, with Ailsa Craig out to sea.

4 At the top go through a kissing gate to the left of the main gate; the latter runs into sheep pens. Carry on along the lovely grassy way contouring the hillside, with fine views down to the right into the valley of the Water of Assel. Go through a small metal gate beside a field gate and cross a bog on a raised path gradually descending into a high valley. Just beyond a waymark post take the left, higher, branch and walk on down to the next waymark. This has 'Girvan' painted on it, with an arrow. Turn left over a bridge which crosses a ditch, and head across the rather wet pasture. Keep high to start with, to avoid a marshy area, then come down to join the obvious path. Cross a wide bog on a raised way, heading for a low signpost where you will find duckboards to cross the wettest part. The path then improves and runs along the side of the hill. Cross a stile and look right to see Laggan Loch, a tiny circular pool with willows along one side.

5 Immediately beyond the stile climb steeply up the bank and then go along the hillside on an indistinct path. Go left to cross above a spring, keeping at this level to join a clearer grassy way which then winds left. Cross a ditch and go through a gap in the embankment beyond. Then pass through a wide gap in a fence and on along the clear track round the hill to a waymark post. Keep straight ahead here. The track becomes stony as it descends, with Dow Hill ahead at first and then on your left as you swing round to the right. In winter the farmer feeds his cattle on the track at the edge of the wood ahead, so you may want to leave the path to its left before you get there and make your way across the rather boggy valley and along the far hillside, to rejoin the track as it runs beside the wood. In summer this will not be a problem. Go on down beside the wood rejoining the path you took up Dow Hill, and retrace your steps to the Shalloch Park car park.

Kestrel

Practicals

Type of walk: *Pleasant walk to the summit of a fine hill (518ft/160m) and on. The paths are delightful grassy ways especially on the highest ground, and the views are excellent. There are waymarks only at the most distant part of the walk and some of those have lost their arrows, but the paths are generally clear.*

Distance:	5 miles/8km
Time:	2–3 hours
Maps:	OS Explorer 317/Landranger 76

Walk 4

Barony Hill from Dailly

Park in the little square or the roadside in the village of Dailly, grid ref 271016. Access the village by the B734 or B741 from Girvan or by the B7203 and B741 from Maybole.

As you stroll beside the Water of Girvan, towards the end of the walk, look up right to see the now derelict **Dalquharran Mansion**. It was built in 1786 to a design by Robert Adam. It was commissioned by Thomas Kennedy who married Jean Adam a niece of Robert Adam. Wings were added to the house in time for a royal visit that never took place. As you wind on along the riverside path you can look across the river to the ruins of Dalquharran Castle surrounded by trees. It dates from the 16th century and was built by a branch of the Kennedys of Culzean.

Dalquharran Castle (the new castle)

1 Leave the square by Main Street in a north-east direction. Continue over Linsayton burn and then cross the road ahead and walk up a surfaced hedge-lined road towards Balcamie Farm. Wind left round the farm. The track becomes rougher, with woodland to the left and

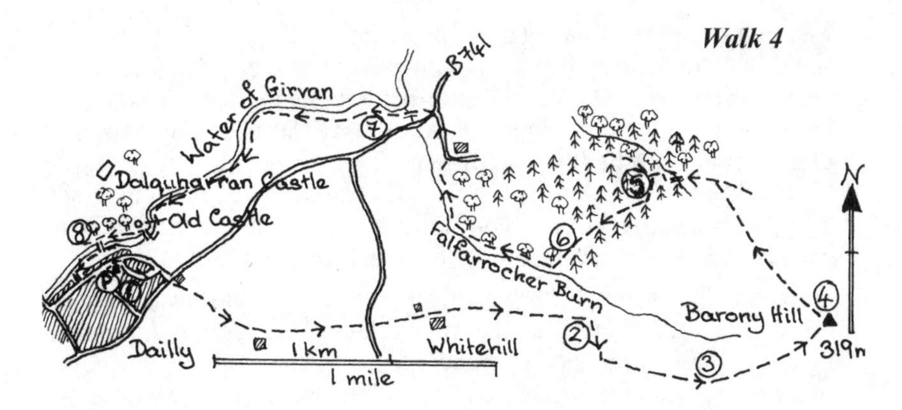

a fine view across to the Maxwellston Hills to your right. Carry on to cross a road and walk ahead on a narrow track. As you pass Whitehill farm on your right, watch for the gap to the left side of an electric tape across the continuing track. Pass through the next gate onto a pleasing grassy track. Beyond the next gate, go ahead up the sloping pasture, beside the wall on your left.

2 Just before the wall ahead, wind round right and walk on to the next wall corner where you might find the way through the short cross wall difficult. If so wind right along the short stretch of wall and curve round its end. Then strike back to the side of the wall on the left, go downhill to cross a ditch to take a sturdy wooden step stile. Beyond look for the prominent waymark on top of a small ridge and head for it. Keep on up beside a deepish ditch to your left and then as you near the barbed wire fence above, cross the wooden plank bridge over the gully and go up to climb the stile over the fence. Walk on up to cross another barbed wire fence by a simple stile.

3 Carry on up a narrower path through the short grass aiming for a most obvious metal waymark, in the form of an oak leaf on a long 'stalk', standing on a small summit. Here there are two ongoing paths, one that winds round the side of the hill and fades, the other crosses a pathless stretch and then becomes distinct as it heads towards this unusual sculpted marker. Walk on along the now distinct path, guided by two more metal waymarks, along the ridge, with incredible views all around. Then you arrive at the trig point (1013ft/320m) and a seat carved from a huge tree trunk.

4 After a pause to enjoy the superb view out to Ailsa Craig and Holy Island and Arran, too, turn left, north-west, and head for the obvious metal waymark. From here you can see the continuing way down the vast high-level moorland. The path can be a little damp in places and sometimes indistinct. But keep on down. At one point the waymark stands on a small hillock and it is difficult to see the route beyond, but keep descending. Soon you join a wide grassy track at a waymark, just after crossing a muddy ditch. The marker directs you, left, to a gate into an area of clear-fell. Here huge wheel ruts dig deep into the track as it winds through an enormous quantity of woodland litter, the way easy to walk when dry. But relief from this desolate spot is at hand.

5 Watch out for a narrow green path, left, which leads you away from all this dereliction, where even the waymark has been knocked out of its hole. The path climbs easily through young birch woodland, the edges of the way lined with heather and where, in late August, guelder rose, blackberry and rowan, laden with berries, thrive, and broom is almost overladen with black seed pods. This is a lovely high-level path that brings you to a clearing, where beech has been wind-blown. Then the path carries on beside woodland to your left and pasture to your right.

6 Climb a wooden hurdle stile to cross a track and take a similar one into mature deciduous woodland. The path is distinct as it takes you down and down through the lofty trees, many of them oak. The way continues for nearly mile, with an accompanying burn deep in its ravine to your left. On reaching a road, turn left and walk down to the main road. Cross over to enter more woodland indicated by a sculpted waymarker showing you where to pass through the lush vegetation of the verge, to continue on a good path. Wind left at the foot of the wood, cross a little bridge and then go on along a stretch of duckboarding. Cross a footbridge from where you have your first glimpse of the Water of Girvan.

7 Stroll on along a narrow path on a raised bank, well above the river. Ignore the bridge across the river and continue on an overgrown path along the embankment of the river above the pasture to your left. Wind left between two huge beeches and then return to the side of the river. As you go look for swallows and sand martins over the water and goldfinches in the bushes. Cross a stile and continue on along the riverside to climb three more stiles. From the last one you have a fine view of the deserted but still very grand Dalquharran mansion. Wind on along the embankment as the river curves, left, passing on the opposite bank the ruined castle of Dalquharran. Carry on to cross a long bridge over the lovely river.

House martin

8 Turn left to walk through fine woodland to cross back over the river on a 'futuristic type' of bridge. Bear right, beyond and stroll on until you can turn left into a wide grassy way that brings you to Main Street. Turn left to return a short way to where you have parked.

Guelder rose

Practicals

Type of walk: *Very satisfying. A great walk of contrasts, mainly on footpaths and tracks. Excellently waymarked.*

Distance: 7 miles/11.5km
Time: 3–4 hours
Map: OS Explorer 326/Landranger 76

Walk 5

Stinchar Falls

Park in Stinchar Bridge car park, grid ref 397957. Access this by an unclassified road between Straiton and Bargrennan.

The falls are quite modest but after rain the water cascades through a series of small waterfalls linked by many of deep pools cut into the rugged rock. The little **River Stinchar** (the ch pronounced as in chain) rises in the Awful Hand Range and after 25miles/40km joins the Firth of Clyde at Ballantrae. As you leave the parking area you see one of the splendid falls on the river. At the flat bridge, point 4, look for the superb fall upstream. It is a pity that the return walk from the flat bridge is in such a poor condition because it is really a lovely way to return rather than along the unsympathetically surfaced forest tracks.

1 From the car park descend right to pass the fine falls on the River Stinchar. Cross the road and walk ahead on a signed narrow reinforced path leading to the falls. This is a solid, slightly raised path but needs care to avoid tripping on the protruding stones. The way passes through a large area of clear-fell that has been delightfully colonised by banks

Falls on Stinchar Burn

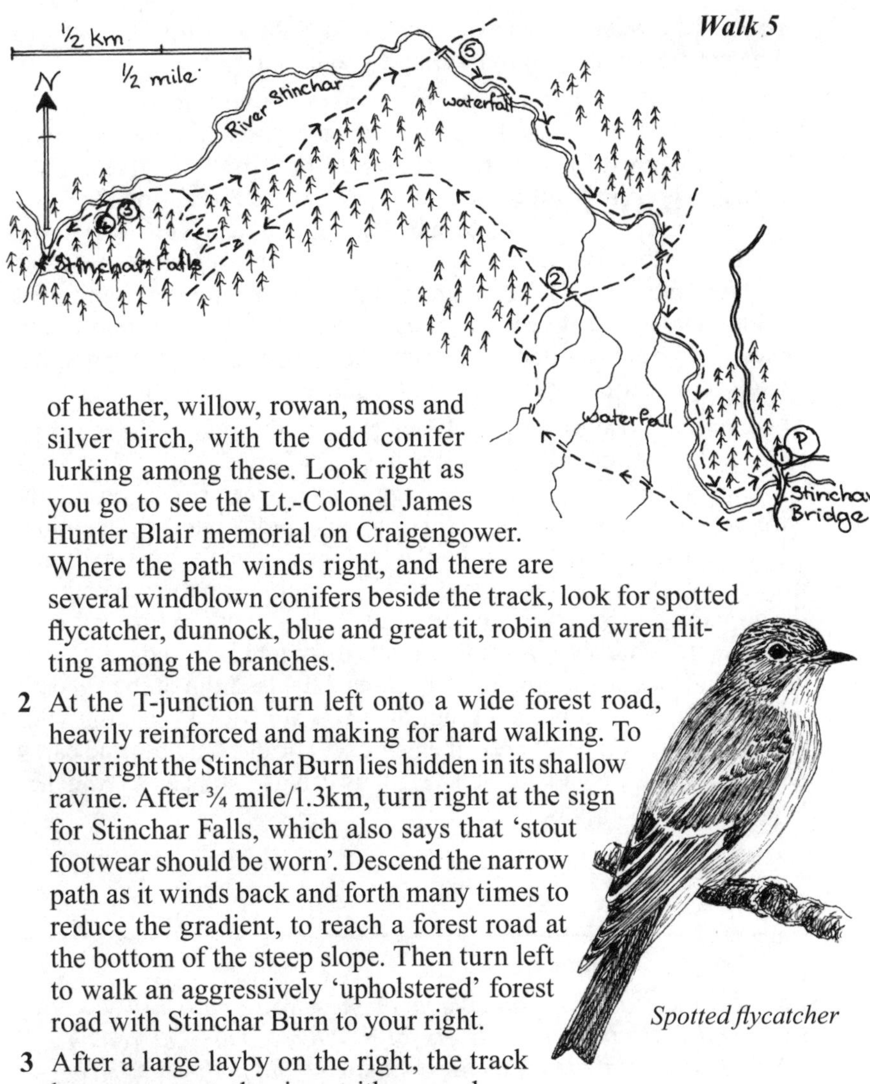

of heather, willow, rowan, moss and silver birch, with the odd conifer lurking among these. Look right as you go to see the Lt.-Colonel James Hunter Blair memorial on Craigengower. Where the path winds right, and there are several windblown conifers beside the track, look for spotted flycatcher, dunnock, blue and great tit, robin and wren flitting among the branches.

2 At the T-junction turn left onto a wide forest road, heavily reinforced and making for hard walking. To your right the Stinchar Burn lies hidden in its shallow ravine. After ¾ mile/1.3km, turn right at the sign for Stinchar Falls, which also says that 'stout footwear should be worn'. Descend the narrow path as it winds back and forth many times to reduce the gradient, to reach a forest road at the bottom of the steep slope. Then turn left to walk an aggressively 'upholstered' forest road with Stinchar Burn to your right.

Spotted flycatcher

3 After a large layby on the right, the track becomes most pleasing, with grass down the middle, larch to the riverside and masses of heather, devil's bit scabious and willow herb to the left. Ahead, over Dunamoddie, you might spot a buzzard being harried by a group of ravens. Beyond a seat, the path narrows and becomes railed as it comes closer to the burn, now very noisy as it races through its deepening ravine. Descend easily into a clump of larch. Follow the little path as it drops right to a fine wooden viewing platform. From here the burn and its cascades are good to see but, alas, the waterfall itself is just out of sight as it tumbles into an even deeper ravine, with trees clinging to its sides.

4 Return up the path to the seat where you might wish to take a break. Look into the larch and sitka, across the path to see families of mixed tits and goldcrest flitting from branch to branch of the trees. Then return along the reinforced road to the foot of the zigzags on the right. Here you have a choice; to return by the route used on your way to the falls. Or, for those experienced walkers who can cope with an almost lost path under overgrown vegetation, go on ahead along the forest road until you cross the Stinchar Burn by a flat bridge. Look upstream to see more cascades and a fine waterfall. Turn right just beyond the bridge onto a narrow path, now with the burn to your right.

5 This once well-cared-for path keeps close to the side of the winding burn. In late summer it is overgrown by lush grass, rushes and great cushions of heather. Many of the boggy patches are crossed on elderly wire-netted planks. There are still waymarks hidden in the vegetation. After a sometimes tedious mile the path brings you to a forest track used as a cycle track, which you cross to continue on the old path. (If the previous section has been very wet, you may wish to turn left onto the cycle track and continue to the road. Turn right here and walk, with care, the ¼ mile to the car park.) The first 220yds/200m of the old path to a small dam is good going but then you are back to picking your way. Cross one very wet area, then a rickety bridge, and beyond carry on between the forest and the river. This brings you back to Stinchar Bridge and the car park.

Practicals

Type of walk: *Rather hard going on the new forest path and wide forest roads. Sturdy shoes or boots for the zigzag path. The return path beyond the flat bridge by the challenging old path needs strong boots and experience at looking ahead to spot the route that is overgrown and where much of the earlier reinforcement is sinking into the rather wet terrain – but it is a lovely path through glorious vegetation, with the delightful burn beside you all the way.*

Distance: 5 miles/8km

Time: 3 hours

Map: OS Explorer 318/Landranger 77

Walk 6

Cornish Hill

Park in the forestry car park at Stinchar Bridge, grid ref 397957, about 6 miles/9.5km south of Straiton along the minor road to Glen Trool and Newton Stewart. Follow the parking signs left along the road to Loch Bradan and the car park is on the left almost immediately after the junction.

The **Galloway Forest Park** is an enormous area of conifer plantations, stretching from Newton Stewart in Galloway most of the way to Straiton and Dalmellington in Ayrshire. The trees are now mostly mature and gradually being felled and parts of the forest are being restructured to make them more attractive. There are many miles of tracks and paths, making the area very good for walking and especially, cycling.

Crossbills are large finches with a heavy bill, the mandibles crossing over at the tip, as the name suggests. This helps them extract the

Falls, Stinchar Bridge

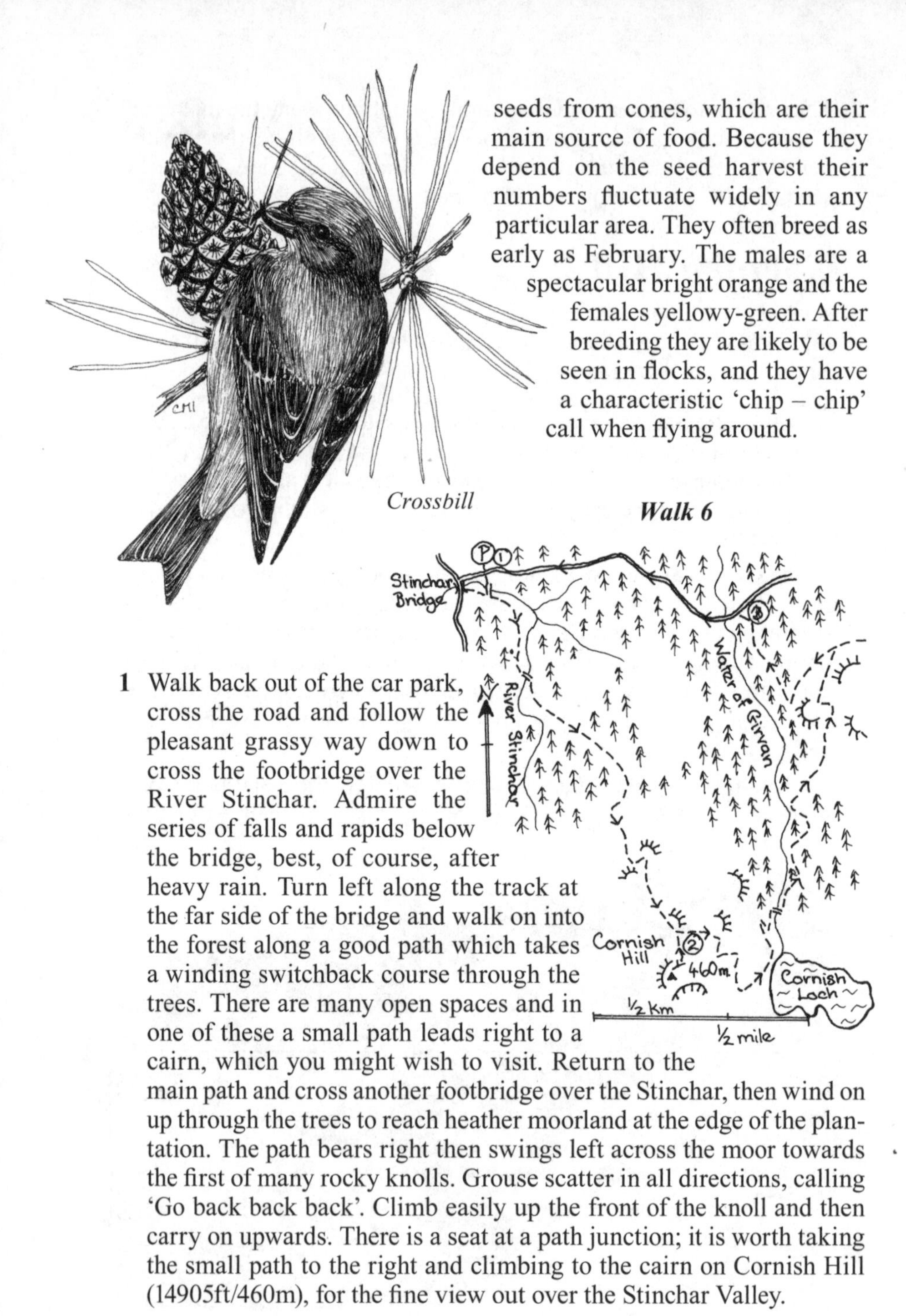

seeds from cones, which are their main source of food. Because they depend on the seed harvest their numbers fluctuate widely in any particular area. They often breed as early as February. The males are a spectacular bright orange and the females yellowy-green. After breeding they are likely to be seen in flocks, and they have a characteristic 'chip – chip' call when flying around.

Crossbill

Walk 6

1 Walk back out of the car park, cross the road and follow the pleasant grassy way down to cross the footbridge over the River Stinchar. Admire the series of falls and rapids below the bridge, best, of course, after heavy rain. Turn left along the track at the far side of the bridge and walk on into the forest along a good path which takes a winding switchback course through the trees. There are many open spaces and in one of these a small path leads right to a cairn, which you might wish to visit. Return to the main path and cross another footbridge over the Stinchar, then wind on up through the trees to reach heather moorland at the edge of the plantation. The path bears right then swings left across the moor towards the first of many rocky knolls. Grouse scatter in all directions, calling 'Go back back back'. Climb easily up the front of the knoll and then carry on upwards. There is a seat at a path junction; it is worth taking the small path to the right and climbing to the cairn on Cornish Hill (14905ft/460m), for the fine view out over the Stinchar Valley.

2 Then return to the seat and turn right to continue along the main path. This now crosses high ground beside a pool, with heather covered heights all round. Wind round another knoll, and suddenly you can see Cornish Loch below you. The path descends in a series of easy zigzags; it is obviously used by mountain bikers as well as by walkers. It swings left just above the water and contours the hillside to the point where a river, the Water of Girvan, flows out of the loch. There are several places along the edge of the loch where you might like to stop for a break. Carry on above the river. As the path approaches the trees again, it bends sharply and follows the outer edge of the forest down to a sturdy footbridge below a shallow gorge. It then runs along beside the river and in and out of the trees. The third time it leaves the river for the trees it begins to climb, and soon you are out on the open heather again. Wind left to climb another knoll, then begin the descent across its face. At a T-junction (unsigned) turn left, although a short detour to the right to the top of the path gives a good view of Loch Bradan. Go down the zigzagging path into larch woodland, the trees well back from the path. Look out for crossbills here, feeding on the cones, and listen for their 'chip chip' call.

3 At the bottom the path comes out on the road to Loch Bradan. Turn left, cross the bridge over the Water of Girvan and carry on along the road for the half mile back to the car park.

Tormentil

Practicals

Type of walk: *Pleasant walk on good paths with fine views from Cornish Hill. Much of the walk is out of the trees on heather moorland. There is a short stretch of road at the end.*

Distance: 3 miles/5km
Time: 2–3 hours
Maps: OS Explorer 318/Landranger 77

Walk 7

Lady Hunter Blair's Walk, Straiton

See walk 8 for parking at Straiton.

The walk is named after **Lady Elizabeth Hunter Blair**, the step-mother of Lt.-Colonel Hunter Blair who died, 1854, at Inkerman in the Crimean War, see Walk 8. She married Sir James Hunter Blair of nearby Blairquhan Castle in the 1840s. The castle, a regency mansion, has, in the past, links with poet, Rabbie Burns, and road builder John Macadam.

Just before you enter Lambdoughty Glen, look right to see the entrance to Largs farm, the home of **Thomas McHaffie**, a covenantor shot dead in 1686. He had been on the run for two years, but illness forced him to hide closer to home. His hiding place was discovered by Andrew Bruce, the infamous hunter of covenanters, and it was his dragoons that shot him. A memorial to McHaffie stands near to the west door of Straiton's church.

When **Dante Gabriel Rossetti** visited the glen he was suffering from insomnia and poor health. As he looked down on Black Linn, now often called Rossetti's Linn, he was so overwhelmed by its beauty, that it is said he thought of throwing himself, suicidally, into the depths.

Straiton

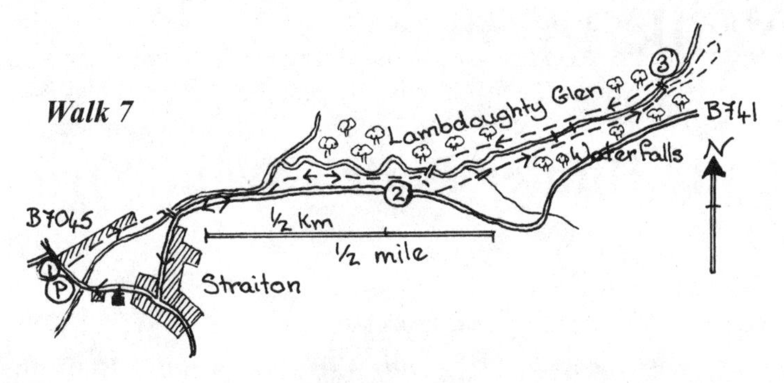

1 Cross the road from the car park and continue along Fowler's Croft, a delightful row of cottages and houses, with a stream hurrying on its way to the right. This pretty development, which is so in keeping with the rest of Straiton, well deserved its award for its architectural design in 1984. Carry on to the end of the houses to cross Sclenteuch bridge onto a road, the B741. Walk left, very soon to follow an arrow that directs you on uphill, but continuing on the left of the hedge that runs on the left side of the road. Head on along this narrow path until you reach the road again. Here look for the arrow directing you into the fine, mainly deciduous, woodland along a good path high above the Lambdoughty Burn.

2 Follow the undulating way that winds below fine trees, some labelled, watching out as you step over tree roots. At a bench seat, there is another entrance to the glen and a small parking area. Wind on round enjoying the sound of the many cascades far below. The flow of the first waterfall, 23ft/7m high and railed, is divided by boulders and falls as long white tresses into a peat-stained plunge pool. Carry on to see a more spectacular fall, Black Linn, 33ft/10m high, often named as Rossetti's Linn. In summer you view it through heavily leaf-laden branches, but in autumn and winter much more of its glory is revealed.

3 Stroll on the pleasing way to reach a footbridge, which you cross to return. Here a plaque explains that the continuing path, now on the opposite side of the burn, was opened in 1994. Follow the path, stepped in places where it rises and falls above the burn. From this side you have a better view of Rossetti's Linn but again through the branches of many trees. Continue on past the lower fall and descend to the side of the hurrying Lambdoughty. Then climb steps up to a fine needle-covered track through conifers. Carry on, gently descending, to a bridge, which you cross. Beyond, follow the path up the slope and bear right to the bench seat at the road entrance once again. Head on right, descending the path taken at the start of the glen walk to join the path inside the hedge. Continue on this until you join the road. Here walk ahead into the village, where you might wish to visit the church, the village stores and post office, The Black Bull Hotel or The Buck for coffee and cakes.

Treecreeper

Practicals

Type of walk: *This is another of Ayrshire's dramatic gorges. The paths are good, but might be muddy after heavy rain. The mixed woodland that covers the steep sides of the gorge is lovely at all times of the year.*

Distance: 3 miles/5km
Time: 2 hours
Maps: OS Explorer326/Landranger 77

Walk 8

The Monument and Bennan Circuit, Straiton

Park in the walkers' car park at Straiton, grid ref 379048. Access the village from the A77 by the B7045.

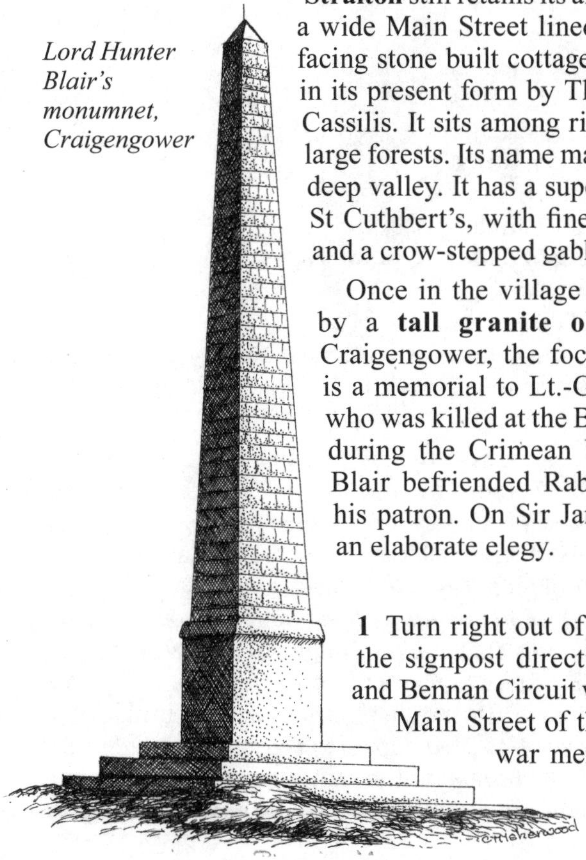

Lord Hunter Blair's monumnet, Craigengower

Straiton still retains its air of a model village, with a wide Main Street lined with rows of opposite facing stone built cottages. It was largely created in its present form by Thomas Kennedy, Earl of Cassilis. It sits among rich agricultural land and large forests. Its name may mean a settlement in a deep valley. It has a superb 18th century church, St Cuthbert's, with fine stained-glass windows and a crow-stepped gable.

Once in the village it seems to be guarded by a **tall granite obelisk** on the hill of Craigengower, the focal point of this walk. It is a memorial to Lt.-Col. James Hunter Blair, who was killed at the Battle of Inkerman, 1854, during the Crimean War. Sir James Hunter Blair befriended Rabbie Burns and became his patron. On Sir James' death Burns wrote an elaborate elegy.

1 Turn right out of the car park and follow the signpost directions for the Monument and Bennan Circuit walk. Continue along the Main Street of the lovely village. At the war memorial bear right as directed by the waymark. Continue on to pass the primary school. Just beyond, take the signed gate onto a wide track and follow it to the top of the sheep pasture and where it winds right to a gate into Traboyack Wood. Climb steadily through conifers, which lie back from the path and allow enough light for the way to be lined with wild flowers. Soon, as the track curves right, conifers crowd in on either side before reaching a gate onto the open hillside.

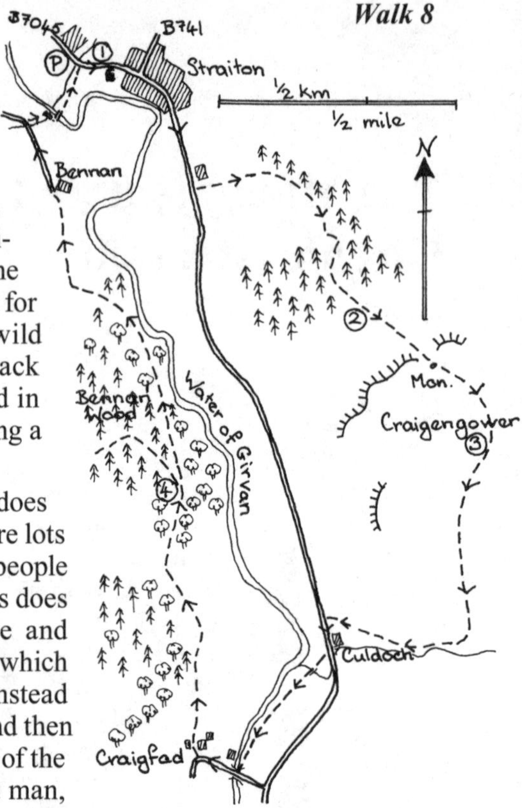

2 Take your climb steadily; it does go up quite steeply. There are lots of 'footsteps' where other people have climbed. The steepness does lessen for a short distance and here ignore the last section, which goes up almost vertically. Instead bear left and climb easily and then wind round right to the foot of the obelisk. (A twenty year old man, in 2010, did both up and down from the monument, in the village race, in 14 minutes.) Enjoy the pleasing views across the glorious countryside to the Firth of Clyde, Ailsa Craig and the mountains of Arran.

3 Then move west to the obvious waymark and follow the grassy trod along roughly the same contour line over the well waymarked ridge. Descend by a track beside a wall, to your left, then move away to cross the field to a gate onto the road at Culdoch. Cross the road and walk left for a few steps to go through a waymarked gate, opposite the cottage. Slant, left, over the pasture to cross a tractor bridge to the side of the Water of Girvan, lined with alders. Go through the next gate to walk a narrow footpath, with a fence to your left and the burn to your right, to climb steps up to the road. Turn right and cross the fine bridge over the burn and continue past Craigfad. Go on to take the next right turn to stroll a grassy track. Continue on through a small plantation to a gate. Beyond, carry on the good path into an open area with a dramatic

view of the monument. Where the paths divide, take the higher one to continue uphill. Climb the low ladderstile and follow the path uphill through dense bracken. Press on through woodland. Cross a little footbridge. Ahead the track leads to the viewpoint on Bennan Hill, which you might wish to attempt, by keeping ahead and then bearing left to the viewpoint.

4 If you have had enough climbing, take the right fork. Leave the woodland and continue through an open area, dropping gently downhill. Once past a huge oak begin to climb the continuing grassy track ahead, with conifers to your right. Head on beyond the gate into a wide open meadow, with a well built wall to your left. At the waymark bear right and descend through a gate. Wind left in front of Bennan farmhouse. Go by the stables. At the three- armed signpost, turn right to pass through a gate and descend beside a small stream with a fence to your left. Cross the stream by a footbridge and, in a few steps, take a second bridge over the lovely river. Stride up the field beside a tributary, with Straiton's fine church ahead. Beyond the next gate, carry on to the road. Turn left over the bridge and walk on to go left again into the car park.

Long-tailed tit

Practicals

Type of walk: *A walk of contrasts, with a steep hill climb where you will enjoy fine views all the way up. The return is made over undulating hills before descending to the Water of Girvan. A pleasing woodland path takes you back to the village.*

Distance:	4½ miles/7km
Time:	3 hours
Maps:	OS Explorer 326/Landranger 77

Walk 9

Ness Glen and Dalcairnie Linn

Park by the Roundhouse Café at the northern end of Loch Doon, grid ref 476012. To reach this leave the A713 about 2 miles/3.3km south of Dalmellington, following signs for Loch Doon, Ness Glen and Galloway Forest Park, and drive for 3 miles/5km to the far side of the dam.

The path through **Ness Glen** was cut through the rock in 1832. However it eventually fell out of use and became dangerous due to landslips and fallen trees. It was completely restored in 2004-5, when the suspension bridge was built and 22 smaller bridges were carried in and installed.

This walk is on the **Craigengillan Estate** and has been made easily accessible to the public. The estate belonged to the Macadams of tarmacadam fame. The house was built in the 1780s and the stone bridge over the River Doon was constructed about this time by French prisoners of war.

Dalcairnie Linn waterfall drops in spectacular fashion over a ledge of rock 20ft/6m into the gorge below. It is said to be possible to walk behind it, but access is difficult and not recommended.

Dalcairnie Linn

Walk 9

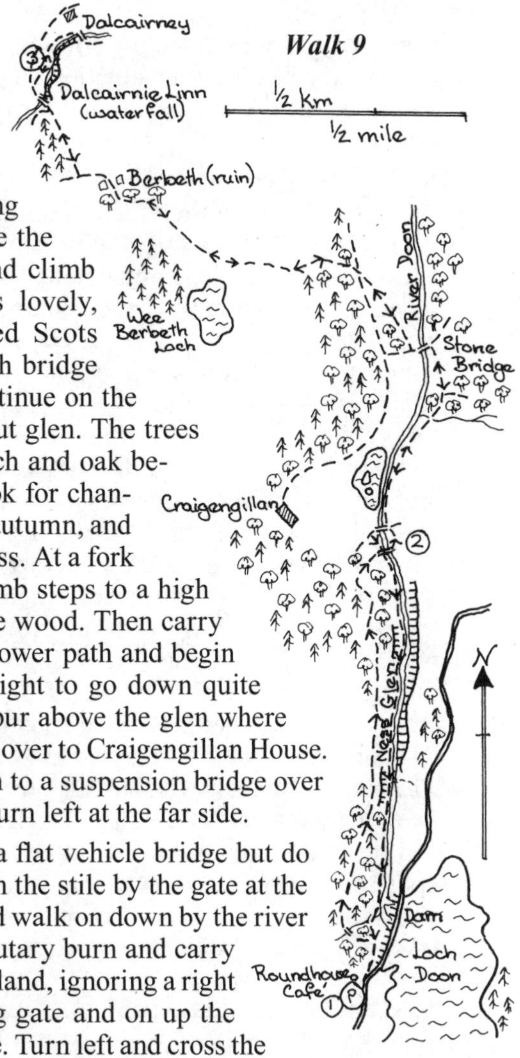

1 Walk back towards the dam and go down the surfaced path on the left of the road, past an information board about Ness Glen. Enter the wood through a metal kissing gate and in a few steps take the left path at a Y-junction and climb the hill. The woodland is lovely, mainly birch with scattered Scots pine and larch. Cross a high bridge over a small ravine and continue on the clear path above the deep-cut glen. The trees change gradually, with beech and oak becoming more common. Look for chanterelles beneath the trees in autumn, and you may see jays flying across. At a fork take the left branch and climb steps to a high viewpoint on the edge of the wood. Then carry on past a seat to rejoin the lower path and begin a gradual descent. Swing right to go down quite steeply, then contour to a spur above the glen where there is another seat looking over to Craigengillan House. Wind round and go on down to a suspension bridge over the River Doon. Cross and turn left at the far side.

2 Walk along by the river to a flat vehicle bridge but do not cross; instead go through the stile by the gate at the opposite side of the track and walk on down by the river through pasture. Ford a tributary burn and carry on along the track into woodland, ignoring a right turn. Pass through a kissing gate and on up the hill, then down the other side. Turn left and cross the fine stone bridge, then turn right after about 25yds/20m to walk a straight track. You may see a great spotted woodpecker here. Cross a metalled drive and go on up through woodland. Go through a kissing gate into a field and follow the track up the left side beside a wood. Beyond the next gate at the top, wind right on a good firm grassy track across a rushy field with Wee Barbeth Loch away to the left. There is mature beechwood beyond the next gate and the ruins of Barbeth. The track goes on round the hillside past a seat, with a fine view out over Bogton Loch down in the valley. Just before the next gate swing downhill (right) through a waymarked kissing gate and descend the field with a plantation on your left. At the end of the trees go through two kissing gates and turn right on a track to cross a stone bridge. Turn right down steps immediately after the bridge for a fine view of the spectacular Dalcairnie Linn waterfall.

3 When you have admired the fall return by your outward route to the flat bridge over the Doon just downstream from the suspension bridge. Cross this and turn left immediately on the far bank. Walk under the suspension bridge and embark on the narrow path through the Ness Glen Gorge. This is an amazing path which skirts the edge of the River Doon, not far above the water in some places. The cliff to your right is hung with ferns and mosses, some of which are rare and which give the gorge the status of an SSSI. The river foams beside you in small falls, rapids and waterslides. There are many bridges and walkways over side burns and in places where the original path has been cut away by the river. In one place the path goes through a gap by a slice of cliff. Do not cross the bridge over the river but keep on the same side. Look for dippers as you go. The banks become lower and less precipitous. Eventually you can see the dam through the trees and the path becomes edged with concrete. Walk uphill away from the river to join your outward path and return to your car. The Roundhouse café just serves takeaway tea and coffee but it may be very welcome.

Greater spotted woodpecker

Practicals

Type of walk: *A delightful river walk, full of interest. Most of the paths are very good, and the gates are in good condition. Not all the paths are waymarked. The section of the walk through the Ness Glen Gorge might be difficult or impassable after prolonged heavy rain, in which case you would have to return by the upper path.*

Distance: 5½ miles/9km

Time: 3 hours

Maps: OS Explorer 327/Landranger 77

Walk 10

Dunaskin, Waterside

The Dunaskin Visitor Centre and the teashop have closed due to lack of funding. The Scottish Industrial Railway Centre, operated by the Ayrshire Railway Preservation Group, is still in business, running Steam Days on summer Sundays, when the large car park will be open. At all other times **park** tidily, nearby on the approach road, grid reference 442084. Avoid blocking access to the huge gates that will be open only on the Steam Days. To reach this site leave the A77, Glasgow to Stranraer, by the A713 at Ayr.

In 1846 **Dunaskin Iron works** was built by Henry Holdsworth and his son John, and it continued producing iron until 1921.The two villages, Lethanhill and Burnfoot Hill, collectively known as The Hill, were built to house the miners who worked the iron-ore deposits close by. When the iron-ore was no longer mined the villagers were not willing to leave and it was not until 1954 that the last resident left.

Old Works, Waterside

Walk 10

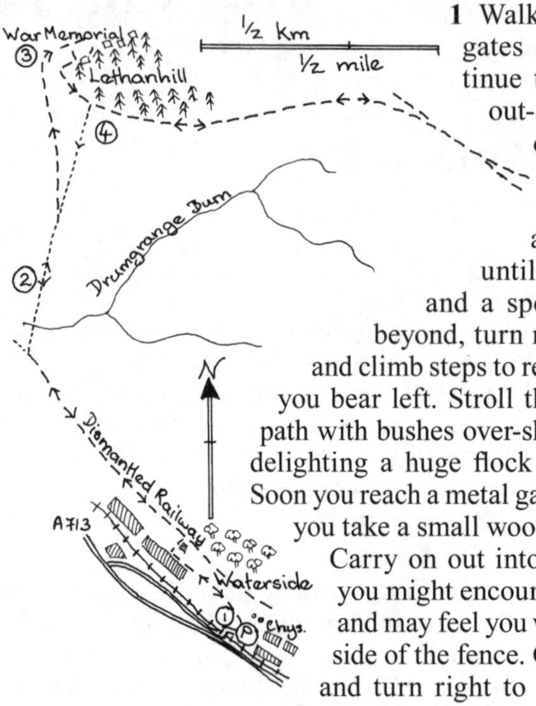

1 Walk the track past the huge gates on your right and continue towards a red signpost, out-of-date generally, but it does direct you to turn left onto a wide track, which is correct. Ignore a right turn, and go on until just past a playground and a sports pitch. A few steps beyond, turn right onto a narrow path and climb steps to reach a grassy trail, where you bear left. Stroll the pleasing flower-lined path with bushes over-shadowing the way, these delighting a huge flock of excited goldfinches. Soon you reach a metal gate across the track where you take a small wooden one to the right side. Carry on out into a large pasture, where you might encounter a large herd of cows, and may feel you wish to divert to the other side of the fence. Go through the next gate and turn right to head uphill over rough ground to pass between the derelict housing of a huge wheel that supported cables, part of the old tramway.

2 Then go on up the steep wide grassy sward. At the top of the slope, pass through two walls, the top end of the housing for the higher wheel of the tramway. Ignore a rather faint right turn and carry on the distinct wide grassy way towards woodland. To your right and in front of this woodland was the deserted village football ground. Where the path is blocked by a fence, wind right to pass through a gate on your left, join a surfaced track and walk right.

3 A few steps along cross, left, on rough ground, to the fenced war memorial naming men from the two villages who lost their lives in the 1914–18 and 1939–45 wars. In front of the memorial stood the village church. Return to the track beside the forest. Peep through the trees to see some remains of the deserted village and go on to come to a white painted memorial, which stands close to the site of the village store. On it, it says 'Long Live The Hill 1851–1954'. Close by was the village square and on the edge of the trees is a ruin, probably the actual store, now almost destroyed by the weather and age.

4 Return along the track to the corner of the wood. Here you might wish to extend your walk for another pleasing 1½ miles/2.5km by turning left along a fine grassy track, a former railway line, with the conifers tightly packed, to your left. As you go look for the remains of what was once Low Row - the houses built for the miners were in rows. Out of one large block of stone large white daisies flower - a poignant spot. Go through a gate and ignore the left turn just beyond. Stroll the splendid level way across the high rolling hills. Here you mighty spot a ginger-coloured fox, with a white tip to its tail, sleeping in the long grass beside the track. Continue on the old track until your way is blocked by corrugated iron. Then return back along the track to the far corner of the wood and turn left to retrace your outward route back to the car park.

Fox

Practicals	
Type of walk: *Fascinating industrial archaeology seen on this walk and the remnants of an old village now almost lost in a small conifer plantation. Good tracks and paths all the way.*	
Distance:	5 miles/8km
Time:	3hours
Maps:	OS Explorer 327/Landranger 77

Walk 11

Croy Bay to Culzean Castle and Country Park

Park in the shore car park at Croy, grid ref 245127. Access this by a narrow lane, off the A719, 9 miles south of Ayr, and just south of the Electric Brae.

Culzean (pronounced Cullain) was given to the National Trust for Scotland in 1945 by the fifth Marquess of Ailsa and the Kennedy family. In 1969 it was declared Scotland's first Country Park. It includes 290 acres of mixed woodland, colourful gardens, pools, streams and a rocky coastline. The spectacular 18th century clifftop castle was designed by Robert Adam.

The fascinating exhibition **in the Gas House by the shore** tells the story of how gas for the castle was produced, and the work of William Murdoch, pioneer of domestic gas lighting.

1 Walk to the end of the car park and descend a narrow roughly stepped slope to the shore. Bear left, south, along the sand and gravel beach, with small low boulder fields that are easy to negotiate. To the left huge red sandstone cliffs, covered with vegetation, rear upwards. Carry on around the lovely bay where, as the tide recedes, oystercatcher, bar-tailed godwit, heron and curlew feed. Enjoy the view across the Firth of Clyde to Holy Island and the Arran mountains, Kintyre and perhaps, Limerick.

2 If the tide has left much slippery seaweed, make use of the intermittent, narrow pebbly

The Gas House, Culzean

path at the top of the beach. Stroll on under more huge sheer cliffs where no plants can gain a hold on the yellow-coloured red sandstone. Eventually you reach two white cottages, Segganwell, on the shore. Go up two steps and walk the grassy way in front of them. Do not go up the dozens of steps behind the cottages. Continue on the good path that crosses a rocky bluff and then runs along the back of the next bay to the fine Gas House. Turn up to see the building and perhaps look at the exhibition.

3 Then carry on upwards using either the steps or the zigzagging road. At the top, bear left onto a road. Almost immediately take the second right turn, which passes under the arch of a viaduct. Continue up to a junction, cross and follow the path to cross another path in a few metres further on. Go up steps towards a deer fence. Stroll left along a narrow path beside the fence. The red deer and some white ones may come quite close. Go to the right up an unsurfaced path between deer fences, which take you right across the Deer Park.

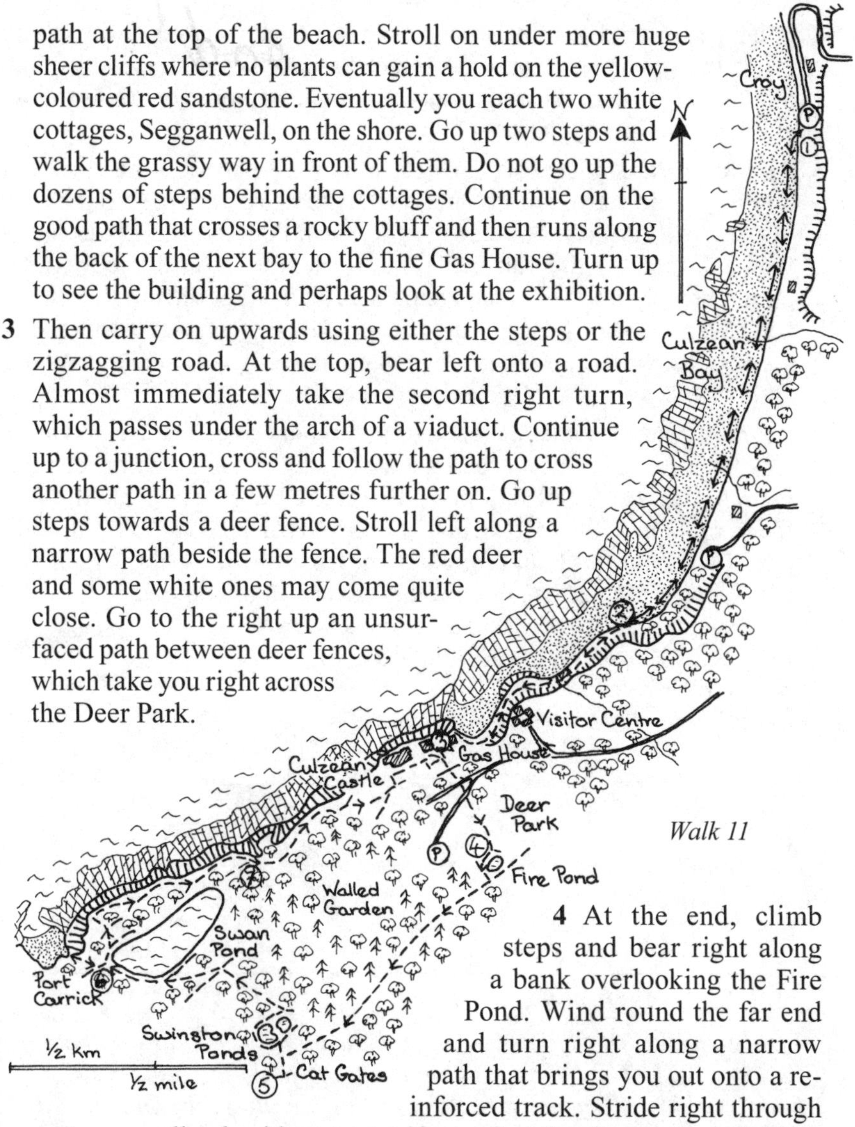

Walk 11

4 At the end, climb steps and bear right along a bank overlooking the Fire Pond. Wind round the far end and turn right along a narrow path that brings you out onto a reinforced track. Stride right through mature woodland, with many conifers at first then increasingly deciduous trees where you might spot siskins. Cross a metalled road and go on downhill. Eventually the road swings round left to the Cat Gates.

5 Turn back on yourself here to take a narrow path on the left (right if you do not go to see the Cat Gates) and then fork left again. Wind round two attractive ponds to reach a T-junction and bear left to round the edge of woodland beside a burn, which eventually spreads into a pond. Cross a major track and go ahead on a path signed 'Swan Pond'. Enjoy this open stretch of water, which has families of swans and many mallards. Go on to the end of the path and carry on over grass to join another path into the trees.

6 At a left turn, signed Port Carrick, follow the path and then go right down steps, to a lovely little sandy bay, where there is a cave at the base of the cliff. Retrace your steps to the Swan Pond and continue round the edge to cross the outflow. Take the next path on the left, which climbs steeply up the wooded bank and turn left at the top to join the Cliff Walk. It winds delightfully in and out of deciduous woodland to viewpoints, with seats, from where you can see Ailsa Craig and Arran, and many seabirds on the stacks and beaches below.

7 Bear left where another path comes in for more splendid coastal views. Go left at the next junction along a wider path that eventually becomes metalled. Ignore a left fork here. The castle becomes visible through the trees. Where the road swings round a sharp bend to the right, walk ahead and into the Fountain Court in front of the castle, which you cross. Enjoy the garden. Go through an arch at the far end and head left to cross a road and go back down to the Gas House, and turn right along the beach to Croy.

Gannett

Practicals

Type of walk: *Mostly level, along a beach and good paths in the Country Park. The beach walking is easiest when the tide is low. In the park there are many paths and you can alter the route to suit your time and preference, but the Cliff Walk should not be missed. There is a Visitor Centre and café, and you can visit the castle (for a fee).*

Distance: 7 miles/11.4km
Time: 3–4 hours depending on the time spent in the park.
Maps: OS Explorer 326/Landranger 70

Walk 12

Dunure

Park on the grassy slopes of the Kennedy Park (small fee) above Dunure Castle, grid ref 251157. The coastal village is signposted off the A719.

Dunure village lies five miles north west of Maybole in South Ayrshire. The fishing village dates from the 19th century, the harbour being improved in 1811. The ruined castle stands on a craggy cliff top hillock. It was built for the Kennedy family (Earls of Cassillis) in the 13th century and several additions were added in the 15th and 16th centuries.

1 From the parking area descend to the dramatic ruined Dunure Castle, which you may wish to visit. Continue north to the 15th century Dovecot. Peep through the grille door to see the nesting sites for the pigeons. Wind on along the path to pass two huge limekilns. Inside you can see lime-loving hart's tongue fern thriving. Follow the arrow directing you to the harbour, winding behind some cottages and then, left, towards the shore path. Bear right to visit the tiny harbour, once a port for sail driven herring boats. Here there are seats to enjoy the view of the wild coastline. Return along the path to pass the castle. Continue over the parkland, along the edge of the cliff, to look down on the recently constructed miniature labyrinth.

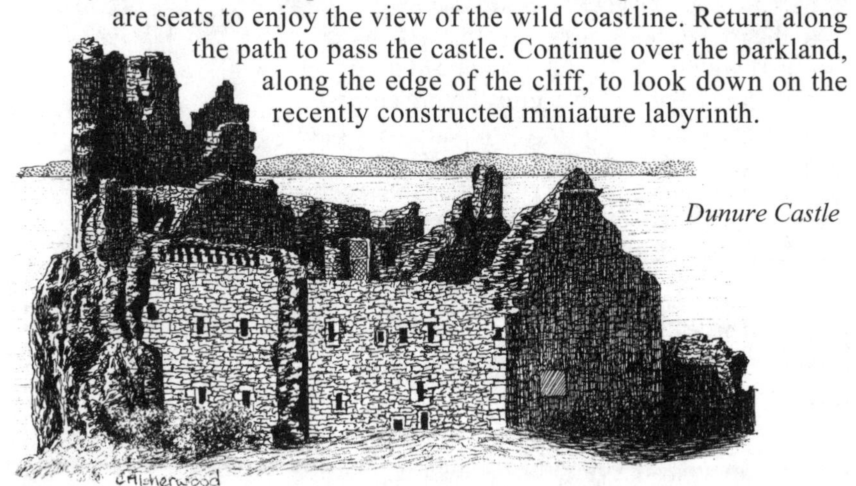

Dunure Castle

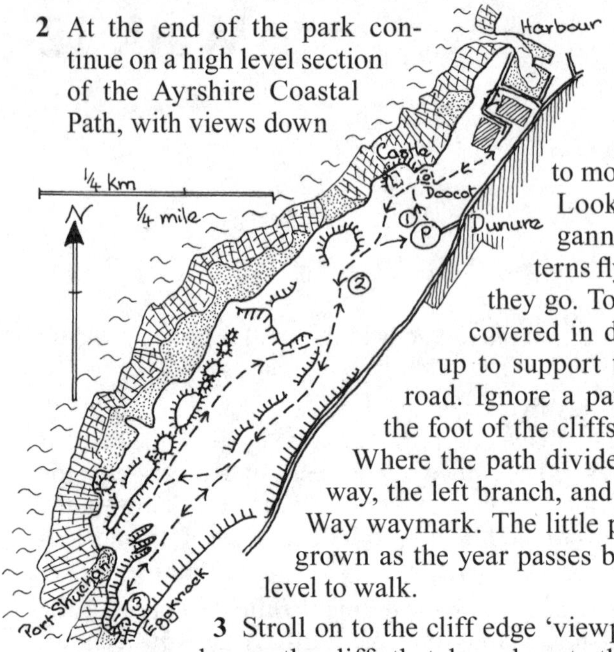

2 At the end of the park continue on a high level section of the Ayrshire Coastal Path, with views down to more of the rocky coast. Look out to sea where gannets dive for fish and terns fly past, 'screaming' as they go. To your left steep cliffs covered in dense vegetation rear up to support the village approach road. Ignore a path that winds left to the foot of the cliffs and carry on ahead. Where the path divides, take the narrower way, the left branch, and head on to a Coastal Way waymark. The little path gets rather overgrown as the year passes but it is still easy and level to walk.

3 Stroll on to the cliff edge 'viewpoint' and, with care, observe the cliffs that drop sheer to the water below. Pause here to look for curlews, oystercatchers and rock doves. Then return to the waymark and go on for a short way to where the path divided. Here turn left, back on yourself and follow the wider path as it drops down to a 3.4km stranded beach and wind left on a narrow path. If you wish to go down to the rocky shore carry on, otherwise wind round with the path and walk ahead until you can wind right, below a crag, before climbing easily to rejoin your outward path. Continue over Kennedy Park to return your vehicle.

Common terns

Practicals

Type of walk: *A delight. Dunure is very interesting and the short walk along the cliffs is most enjoyable.*

Distance: 2 miles/3.4km
Time: 1–2 hours
Maps: OS Explorer 326/Landranger 70

Walk 13

Alloway and Rabbie Burns

Start from the Greenan car park, close to the beach at Doonfoot, grid ref 317194. To access this take the A719 south from Ayr town centre and turn right at the Doonfoot roundabout and continue to the shore.

Robert Burns, poet, lyricist and national poet of Scotland, (widely known by his informal forename Rabbie) was born January 25th 1759 in Alloway, two miles south of Ayr. He was the eldest of seven children born in a house built by his father, a self-educated tenant farmer. The house is now Burns Cottage Museum. Rabbie lived here for seven years and then the family sold the house and moved to a farm, south-east of Alloway. Here they lived in poverty and did severe manual labour which had a detrimental effect on the future poet's health.

Greenan Castle

The poem **Tam o' Shanter** was written by Burns in 1790. It tells the story of a man, Tam, who stayed too long at a public house in Ayr. Kate his wife prophesied that one day his drinking would end with his being found dead in the River Doon. After a lengthy session in the pub, Tam begins his long ride home through the lonely Ayr countryside. As he nears Alloway Kirk he sees it flooded with light and witches and warlords dancing, an open coffin and the Devil. One witch begins to throw off her clothes and

Tam, so beguiled, lets out a loud whoop. Suddenly all becomes dark and Tam races away on his mare, Meg, realising that once across the Doon by the old bridge he'd be safe – witches and warlocks cannot cross running water. Tom and Meg just make the middle of the bridge when Nannie, the first of the witches chasing him, grabs the mare's tail, which comes off.

Walk 13

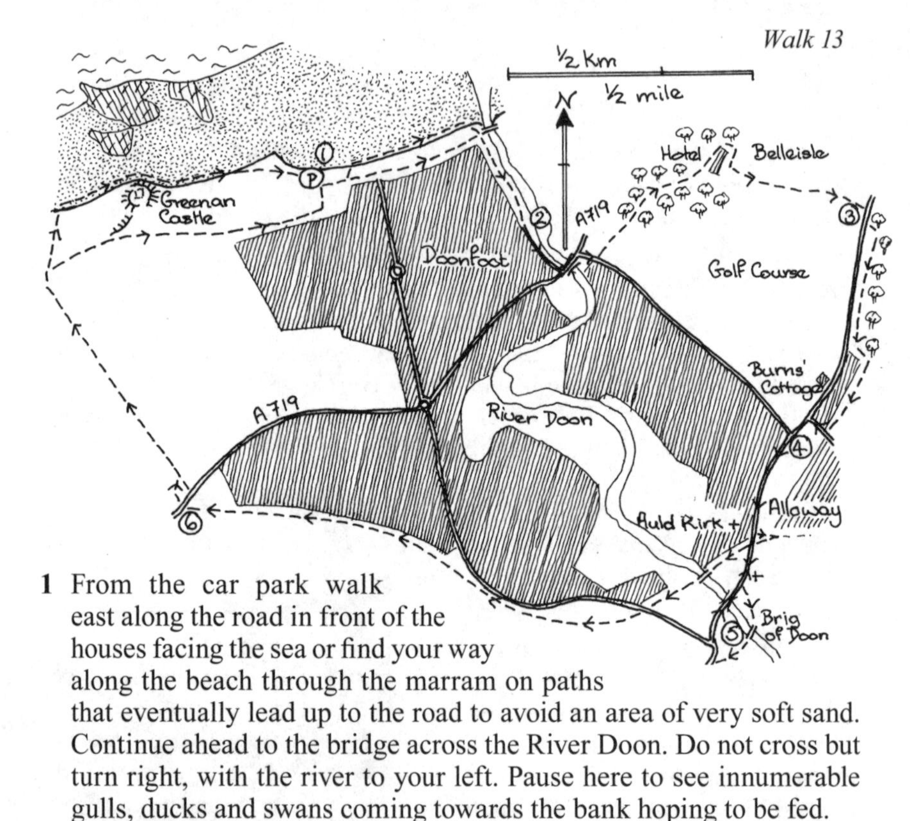

1 From the car park walk east along the road in front of the houses facing the sea or find your way along the beach through the marram on paths that eventually lead up to the road to avoid an area of very soft sand. Continue ahead to the bridge across the River Doon. Do not cross but turn right, with the river to your left. Pause here to see innumerable gulls, ducks and swans coming towards the bank hoping to be fed.

2 Continue along Scaur o' Doon Road until you reach the busy A719. Walk left for a few steps to continue over the road bridge above the River Doon. Cross the A-road, with care, and turn right into Greenfield Avenue to stroll the left side. Where it soon winds right, go through gates into Belleisle Park. Stride the tarmacked track, with the golf course to the right, and then, very shortly, take a narrower unsurfaced path, right, into woodland. Follow the path, steadily arcing round left, beside a high wall and then through a glorious garden, with a huge old greenhouse to your right. Climb the path slanting uphill towards a car park. Go past the front of Belleisle House Hotel and turn right to wind beside, and then behind, the attractive building to come to a notice directing you, left, to the 'Practice Area', a long wide track dividing two golf courses.

3 Pass through green iron gates and carry on right along a tree-lined road. A short way along, cross to enter Rozelle Park. Immediately turn right along a pleasing bridlepath through glorious forest trees. After ¼ mile/0.5km look for a narrow path, right, to take a few steps to the corner of Well Park road and press on along it to turn right, and then left, into the main street of the lovely village of Alloway. Bear left to pass the thatched cottage where Rabbie Burns was born and which is now a museum. The charming cottage lies on the opposite side of the road if you wish to visit.

4 Continue on down the main street, to reach the Auld Kirk, on the same side as the cottage. Wander around the tiny ruin and through the interesting gravestones and remember Tam's experience. Look for those of Burns's parents who were buried here. Return across the road to reach the parish church, which you might also like to visit. Beyond, stroll left to visit the fine Grecian-style monument set in its splendid gardens. Here you will want to sit a while and then visit the fascinating tiny building, the Statues House. Walk on from here and descend steps on the right to the foot of Brig of Doon. As you cross the splendid single-arch remember that it was here that Tam o' Shanter's horse lost its tail.

5 Continue over the bridge and go on up the signed overgrown path to pass under an old bridge and, at the top, turn right to join the B7024. Walk right to cross the fine road bridge over the Doon from where there are splendid views of the Brig of Doon. Carry on up past the two churches and Burns's Cottage and continue until you can turn right into Murdoch's Lone opposite the Tam o' Shanter Experience. Immediately take the signed steps, on the left, down to the old railway track and turn left to pass through a long, well-lit tunnel. At its end, stride the surfaced hedged track for nearly 2 miles/3.4km, out into pleasing open countryside to reach the A719.

6 Cross with care and a couple of steps left, take a signed footpath and bear right. At the surfaced road, turn left to walk the undulating way between fields and often shaded by forest trees. Eventually it becomes an easy-to-walk track. Watch out for where it winds sharp right, and take, just beyond the right-hand bend, a signed footpath heading towards the beach, passing through lush vegetation. Turn right to walk the sandy way. Keep left of a large pool and walk on below the huge cliff on which stands the ruin of Greenan Castle where you will want to have your camera handy. Wind round the great crag. (If the tide is very high you will have to wait for it to recede, or return to the track corner and continue on, left along the track until you can turn left to the Greenan car park.) Carry on along the beach and turn right to the car park when you can see a wide track heading right through the marram grass.

Gulls (black-headed)

Practicals

Type of walk: *Almost level all the way. A mixture of road walking and delightful surfaced track walking.*

Distance: 7½ miles/12km
Time: 3–4 hours
Maps: OS Explorer 326/Landranger 70

Walk 14

Beside the River Ayr

Park in the Riverside car park, grid ref 343218, north side of the Ayr River in the centre of Ayr.

The county town of Ayr, situated at the mouth of the River Ayr, has held **royal burgh** status since 1205. It was in the hands of the English from 1301 to 1312. In the 16th century part of the town was used as a fortress by Cromwell's men. He built a huge wall round sections of the town, some of which can be seen today.

Towards the end of this walk you cross a fine green painted footbridge, donated by a brewer in the Victorian days to help his workers. Pause half way across to look downstream towards the **Auld Brig**. It replaced a timber bridge and was rebuilt in stone in 1470. In 1910 it was rebuilt. Today it is used as a pedestrian bridge. In 1788 a new bridge was built on the line of an old ford – perhaps the earliest crossing of all. The new bridge was washed away in 1870 by flooding and, until it was replaced in 1878, the Auld Brig came into its own again.

Auld Brig, Ayr

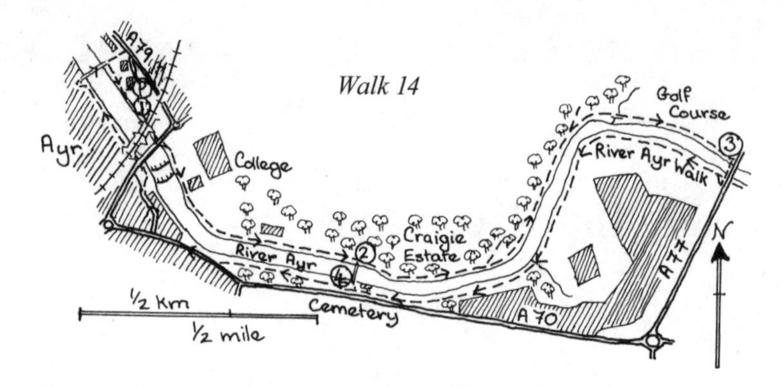

1 Walk from the car park to the nearby riverside and look for goosanders mingling with gulls on the water. Turn left to follow the wide track. Pass below the fine railway bridge and then a road bridge. Beyond, notice the two weirs, which hold back the tide and fish ladders for the salmon to pass upstream. Continue beside well-tended flowerbeds and lawns in front of a very modern university building. Then the good track leads you into fine woodland, with large forest trees on either side, through which you can see the river surging, peat stained, towards the sea. When you have a choice of tracks or paths, take the one to the right.

2 Ignore the fine footbridge over the river and carry on the path as it moves into trees again, remaining close to the Ayr. Across the water, fly fishermen wade into the river after an elusive salmon. At the next Y-junction, take the right fork, a narrow path beside the tree-lined river, with the golf course to your left. Watch out for golf balls. Eventually the path leads up a little slope to join the A77.

3 Turn right to cross the bridge, Overmills Bridge, where you have a barrier to keep you safe from the hurrying traffic. Bear right at the other end and descend steps to the opposite bank of the Ayr to join the River Ayr Walk. Pass through more trees and then the way opens up to the left and the extra light has encouraged a multitude of wild flowers, including yellow loosestrife, meadow cranesbill and soapwort. The path then moves into woodland and goes past a large building, an old three-kiln that dates back to around the 1750s. It was used to burn limestone, converting it to lime to be used as a soil conditioner as well as in the iron industry. Here a plaque states that the River Ayr Walk was opened in 1910 by James Hunter in memory of his older brother.

4 Ignore the bridge across the river, which you saw on your outward route, and carry on gently climbing to a wide grassy area with seats and a road beyond, to the left. Move into more trees until you have to pass through a purpose-built gap in the wall to your left to join the road. Walk on a short way to take the first right turn, Mill Brae, and wind round right and down towards the river. Pass through a car park and descend to the waterside and the weirs to join a path and turn left. Pass under the road bridge and then the railway bridge with its three fine abutments and walk on along the riverside to cross the new footbridge. Half way across look downstream to see the Auld Brig so liked by Rabbie Burns and perhaps read his poem 'The Brigs of Ayr'. At the far side turn right and walk upstream to regain the car park.

Kingfisher

Practicals

Type of walk: *Almost all on good wide tracks, close to the river. A lovely green corridor through the town of Ayr and beyond.*

Distance: 4 miles/6.5km
Time: 2–3 hours
Maps: OS Explorer 326/Landranger 70

Walk 15

Oswald's Bridge to Wallace's Seat

Park in one of several laybys, east of Oswald's Bridge, grid ref 387232. Access this from the Ayr by-pass to take the B743 towards Auchincruive. After ½mile/1km take a minor road right and continue to cross Oswald's Bridge.

Oswald's Bridge was built in 1826 as an estate bridge replacing a much older one. It is believed that William Wallace once hid in the woods here. The earth path takes you beside the lovely River Ayr through trees and on a sunny day through dappled shade.

1 Walk back towards the bridge and just before it, take steps on the right to descend to a good footpath, as directed by a green arrow. Walk on the railed way with the River Ayr to your left, with retrospective glimpses of the glorious bridge. Beyond the rail the bank drops steeply down to the river, with lush vegetation covering the slope and fine forest trees shadowing the river. On passing a huge ancient horse chestnut tree and before an old fishing hut, take a stile over the barbed wire fence into a field and walk along the side of it, still with the river to the left. Continue across the pasture to the next stile and climb back over the fence.

2 Carry on above the river under more magnificent beech, climbing to join a track. Turn left and walk on with a ravine to the right through

Oswald's Bridge

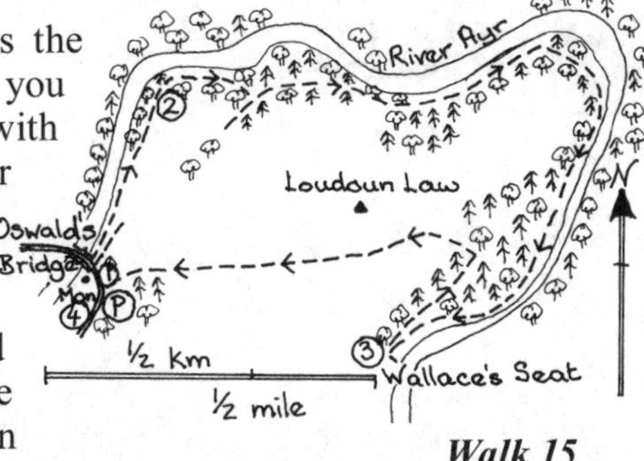

Walk 15

which runs a footpath. As the track continues it brings you to the side of more fields, with the river now hidden far below. Join the River Ayr Way and follow it, left, walking below an avenue of Scots pine. Descend gently and you can see the river through the trees. Then you come close beside it where you might spot dipper and heron. Climb steadily under more beech and ascend steeply, the steps railed on the riverside at the steepest part.

3 Walk on a short way to descend, on the left, a steep railed slope to Wallace's Seat and a viewpoint of the lovely river. This is believed to be where William Wallace sat and planned his fight against the English. After a pause here, climb back up the steep slope to the main track and walk right for a short way to take a wide grassy trod, to the left of the path you ascended. At a junction with a track, turn left. The way moves out of the trees and passes through pastures on either side. Go through a gate and continue on to a gate onto the road close to where you have parked.

Heron

4 Nearer the bridge look for an ornate iron gate that gives access to a memorial cairn dedicated to Robert Burns and William Wallace by the Robert Burns World Federation. A short distance further along steps lead down to the river and from the foot of these you have a good view of the old bridge. Have your camera handy.

Practicals

Type of walk: *Most pleasing. Along the side of the River Ayr on good paths that will be muddy after rain.*

Distance: 3 miles/5km
Time: 1–2 hours
Maps: OS Explorer326/ Landranger 70

Walk 16

Ayr Gorge

Park in the layby opposite the Failford Inn or continue a few yards along the road to another layby, grid ref 461262. Access this by turning east off the A77 onto the A719 and then immediately right, south, onto the B742. At Mossblown continue on the B743.

The **Ayr Gorge** is part of the much larger Scottish Wildlife Trust reserve and a Site of Special Scientific Interest (SSSI). The River Ayr starts from the western shore of man-made Glenbuck Loch and joins the Ponesk burn in East Ayrshire before continuing on its way to the Atlantic. At Failford it begins its journey through the dramatic Ayr Gorge.

Steps, Ayr Gorge, Failford

In the year 1785 Robert Burns had fallen in love with Mary Campbell (**Highland Mary**) whom he had seen at church. In 1786 they plighted their troth over the Water of Fail – a traditional form of marriage. Soon afterwards Mary visited her parents in Campbeltown and together they visited her sick brother in Greenock. He had typhus and Mary caught it on her visit and died later that month.

On the 14th May, 1786 Robert Burns and Highland Mary took their **last farewell**. On a delightful small hillock overlooking the Fail Inn stands a monument with the following poem by Burns:

That sacred hour
can I forget.
Can I forget the
hallowed grove
Where by the winding
Ayr we met
To live one day of
parting love.

This walk uses good paths sometimes close to the **peat-stained river** and sometimes high up along the top of the gorge. They take you through magnificent deciduous woodland where beech, larch, ash or birch shadow the way. Through the trees slip coal tits, goldcrests, and long tailed tits. There are several long flights of steps but these are well-made and easy to ascend or descend.

Walk 16

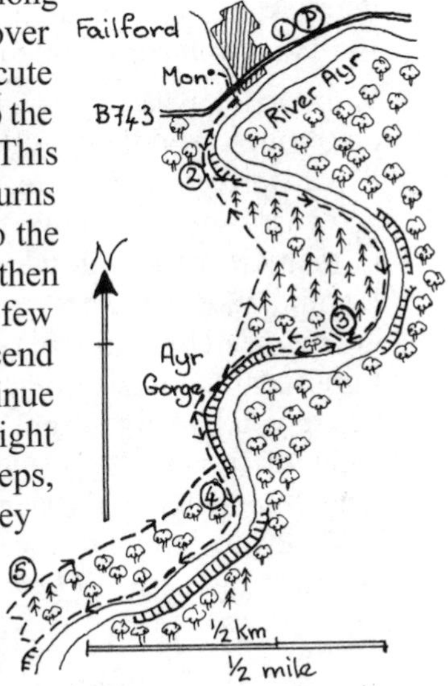

1 From where you have parked, walk back along the road in the direction of Ayr, continue over the bridge and immediately take an acute right, unsigned path to steps leading up to the monument standing on a grassy ridge. This commemorates the parting of Rabbie Burns from his love, Highland Mary. Return to the road, cross over a tributary stream and then cross the road, with care, and carry on a few steps to the entrance to the gorge. Descend the path, go over a footbridge and continue to the foot of a flight of steps on the right and the river to your left. Climb the steps, taking your time, and follow them as they wind round left at the top of the gorge. Walk on a very short way to reach an acceptable bench seat where you can sit and get your breath back. Notice behind the bench a narrow path going straight up to a wider track and then continuing up another slope to another wider track – this is your easily-missed return track.

2 From the seat continue on the same undulating path through the glorious woodland, before gradually descending to the side of the stately river overshadowed by high rock walls. Continue on to reach a division of the ways and take the left branch, continuing ahead until the path ends at a wooden viewing platform at the base of a wonderful red rock staircase carved into the sheer sandstone rock face. It was here that Alexander Peden, a 17th century Covenanter, preached to his followers.

3 Return to the junction and turn left. Soon the path begins to climb steadily through the fine woodland and brings you to the side of farmland. Here bear left, descend to cross a little footbridge and carry on for a short way beside the open countryside. To your left very steep slopes drop to the river, which in summer is hidden from sight by the lush vegetation. Youngsters should be reminded to keep away from the edge. Stroll on the lovely way to another seat, above a long flight of steps. Here might be the place for your picnic.

4 Go down the steps and follow them as they wind right and on down to the riverbank. Carry on downstream, the river passing below enormously high tree-clad cliffs, where you might spot a heron and several dippers. At the end of the path ascend another long flight of steps leading away from the river and up the side of the gorge to reach a stile on the left into pasture. This is the route of the long distance footpath, the River Ayr Way, which goes on towards the sea. This walk turns right.

5 Walk on the pleasing way with open countryside to your left and then on through woodland, retracing your earlier steps to reach a junction of paths. Keep ahead here, ignoring the right turn (your outward route) and carry on high above the Ayr. Eventually you pass a small cairn in memory of a man who lost his life in an accident. Beyond, ignore the first small right turn and go on, watching for a second narrow right turn that leads to the bench seat where you rested in point 1. Turn left and retrace your steps to descend the long flight down to the side of the river. Turn left to return to the B-road, where you turn right.

Goldcrest

Practicals

Type of walk: *A lovely walk on good paths. There are several long flights of steps from the top of the gorge to the river and in the opposite direction. The treads are all in good condition and easy to use.*

Distance: 4 miles/6.5km

Time: 3–4 hours

Maps: OS Explorer 326/Landranger 70

Walk 17

Lord Bute's Walk and the Lugar Water

Park in the walkers' car park, grid reference 543212, on the Dumfries House Estate. To reach this take the B7036 which runs between Auchinleck and Ochiltree and turn off to the south immediately to the west of the A76 road bridge, following signs for Dumfries House. Drive through the gateway (the gates are locked at 6pm or dusk, whichever is earlier, so take care) Go past a cottage and a children's playground, then turn left up a signed track. The car park is on the right.

The small town **Auchinleck** was the home of James Boswell, the 9th Laird of Auchinleck, best known for his biography of Samuel Johnson. To the west of the town stands the Barony A frame, the last remnant of the Barony Colliery. This was the main frame that operated the cages to lower miners into the pit. The area around it is now a picnic area and there are interesting panels about the mine. One plaque commemorates four miners who died as a result of an accident.

Dumfries House was built in the 1750s by the Adam Brothers for William Dalrymple, the 5th Earl of Dumfries. It was inherited, eventually, by the Marquesses of Bute and lived in by the family until 2007. This walk was Lord Bute's favourite walk.

CHilderwood

Avenue Bridge, Lugar Water

Bello Water and Guelt Water both flow from the Southern Uplands in east Ayrshire. They combine to form the **River Lugar**. It journeys through the Dumfries estate and flows beneath the beautiful Avenue Bridge. After 20 miles it joins the River Ayr. There are paths by the Lugar all the way to Ochiltree, the next village.

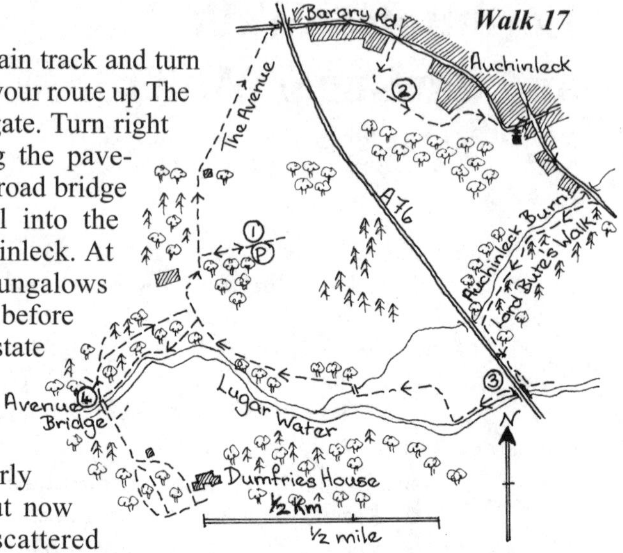

Walk 17

1 Return to the main track and turn right, retracing your route up The Avenue to the gate. Turn right and walk along the pavement under the road bridge and up the hill into the village of Auchinleck. At the brow the bungalows stop. Turn right before the industrial estate and follow the obvious path to the top of the low hill, formerly a spoil heap but now grassy with scattered trees. The view from the top out over the Lugar valley is splendid, with the Arran hills as a distant backdrop. The Barony A Frame is clearly visible nearer to.

2 Continue along the top and then go down the distinct path. Bear left at the foot, towards old mine winding gear. Go under or round it and on along the path at the edge of a car park, to rejoin the road. Walk on towards Auchinleck Parish Church, where the road makes a right-angled bend. Continue down to the traffic lights and turn right opposite the Boswell Arms. Beyond a garage the road crosses the Auchinleck Burn in a deep ravine. A few steps further on turn right through new fencing and a gateway to walk along Lord Bute's Walk. This is a lovely path along the side of the ravine through Scots pine and beech trees with the burn far below. Gradually descend to the level of the burn, then the by-pass comes into view ahead and the path swings left. Carry on with fields to your left and young trees between you and the road to the right. The path moves away from the road into a young plantation. At a junction take the path through the kissing gate on the right and go on down to the bank of the Lugar Water.

3 Turn right and walk under the road bridge, and then on by the attractive river. You may scare a heron, or see a goosander diving for fish. The path suddenly moves inland away from the riverbank and skirts a large marshy area with fields on the other side. Cross an interesting footbridge, wind round a copse of mature oaks and then walk along the edge of woodland, with glimpses through the trees of Dumfries House on the far side of the river. The path bends away from the river and heads towards a distant farm. Before you reach the end of the wood, look for a path leading left into the trees and follow it back to the river bank. Look for both nuthatches and tree creepers here, and you may see a jay. There is a seat made out of a tree trunk which would be a lovely place to stop for a snack.

4 A short way along you reach a splendid bridge over the river. The path passes under it and then turns right to come out onto a track. If you want to visit Dumfries House, which is open from April to October, turn right, cross the bridge and bear left. Otherwise turn left and follow the track round to the right, ignoring two left turns, until you reach the end of the wood. Swing round to the left and head up to the farm. Carry on to the right with a wooden stockade fence to the left. Wind round left to a track junction and turn right to return to the car park.

Nuthatch

Practicals

Type of walk: *Pleasant. Through lovely woodland and pastures. The gates and bridges are all new and the paths clear.*

Distance: 3 miles/5km

Time: 1–2 hours

Maps: OS Explorer 327/Landranger 70 and 71

Walk 18

Afton Reservoir

Park in the large car park provided by Scottish Water, grid ref 628054. To reach this, take the minor road, Afton Road, running south from the B741 at the western edge of New Cumnock. The minor road is narrow and potholed, but the valley is very beautiful. Drive on for 8 miles/13km to the Water Filter Station. Keep straight ahead here, ignoring the more obvious branch which curves round into the Filter Station. Cross a bridge and drive along a track into a plantation. The car park is on the right. If for any reason it is not available there is plenty of parking along the road before the Filter Station. Scottish Water asks that you park with consideration and do not block the entrances or roadways.

The source of **Afton Water** is on the slopes of Alwhat Hill, south of New Cumnock. It flows due north for eight miles, eventually flowing into the Nith near the village. One of Robert Burns's most popular songs is 'Afton Water'. This is the first verse:

> Flow gently, sweet Afton among thy green braes,
> Flow gently, I'll sing thee a song in thy praise:
> My Mary's asleep by thy murmuring stream,
> Flow gently, sweet Afton, disturb not her dream.

Afton Reservoir

Walk 18

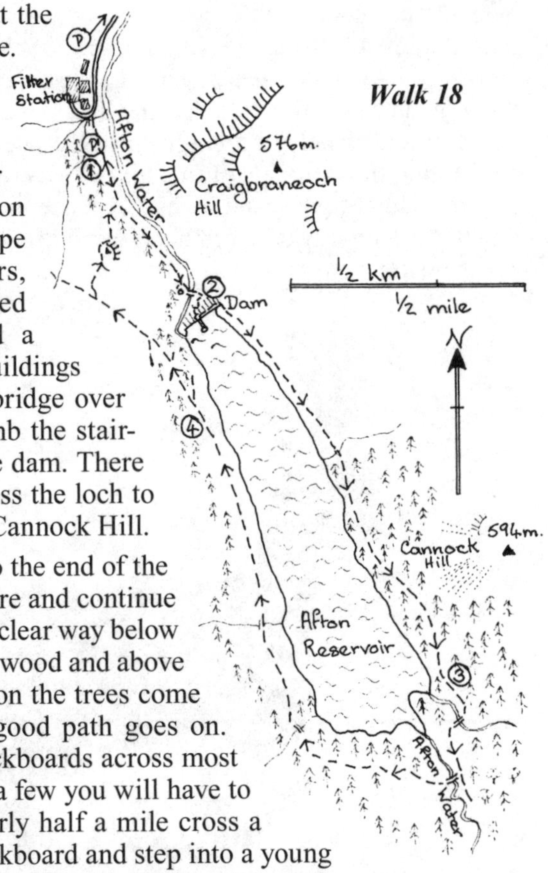

1 Leave the car park at the far end, by a small gate. Carry on towards the reservoir, with the little falls and rapids of the Afton Water below to your left. Soon the high, grassed slope of the dam appears, with a fine staggered staircase up it and a fountain and other buildings in front. Cross the bridge over the outflow and climb the staircase to the top of the dam. There is a lovely view across the loch to the hills, especially Cannock Hill.

2 Turn left and walk to the end of the dam. Cross a stile here and continue to the right along the clear way below the edge of a conifer wood and above the water's edge. Soon the trees come to an end, but the good path goes on. There are sturdy duckboards across most of the wet areas but a few you will have to negotiate. After nearly half a mile cross a low fence with a duckboard and step into a young plantation. The trees are scattered and well back from the path, which contours above the loch. At first it is quite wet, but soon joins an old forest track after which the surface improves. The woodland is of mixed age with patches of mature conifers separated by younger trees. You may see roe deer or a kestrel hovering.

3 Go downhill towards the end of the loch and wind round with the path to cross a concrete bridge. Then take a right fork over another concrete bridge across the Afton Water and walk on into mature woodland. Look and listen for crossbills here. Beyond a cattle grid the trees stop and you enter an area of old clear-fell where young trees are colonising. There are fine views across the loch to Cannock Hill and Craigbraneoch Hill on the far side.

4 The path rises slightly and runs back into trees. Ignore a right turn. Press on the high level way with the dam now visible through the trees below you. Cross a cattle grid by a signpost to come out of the trees onto the open hillside and join another track. Descend slightly until you reach a wooden sheep pen. Here take a waymarked path just before it and wind round the far side. The hillside is dotted with spectacular boulders and ahead is a rock-girt hillock. The path becomes indistinct but keep to the near side of this hillock where it becomes clear again, curving round to descend by an old fence to a stile. Cross and go on down the steep way to rejoin the reservoir road at the bottom. Turn left and return to your car.

Roe deer

Practicals

Type of walk: *An enjoyable relatively level walk round a beautiful reservoir. The area feels very remote, but the paths are clear and waymarked. The first part along the side of the reservoir can be wet in places, but mostly has duckboards.*

Distance: 4½ miles/7km
Time: 2–3 hours
Maps: OS Explorer 328/Landranger 77

Walk 19

Cairn Table

Park in the walkers' car park, grid ref 696265, south of Muirkirk. To access this leave the A70 along a minor road at the south-west end of the village, following signs to the car park. Go through the gap where the railway once crossed the road and turn left into the car park.

Hen harriers are beautiful birds of prey and are probably the most persecuted of all raptors in this country, largely because they are thought to take grouse chicks, although their main diet is small rodents. Where they thrive they are wonderful to watch, hunting low over the moors with wings held in a shallow V or indulging in an aerobic display in spring, which has earned them the name 'sky-dancer'. Later you may spot the silver-grey male bringing food for the brown 'ring-tail' female and passing it to her in flight; she may even turn on her back to catch it. They are protected on the moors round this area and a watch is kept. If you see anyone you think is trying to harm the birds you are asked to report it. The number to ring is given on the notices.

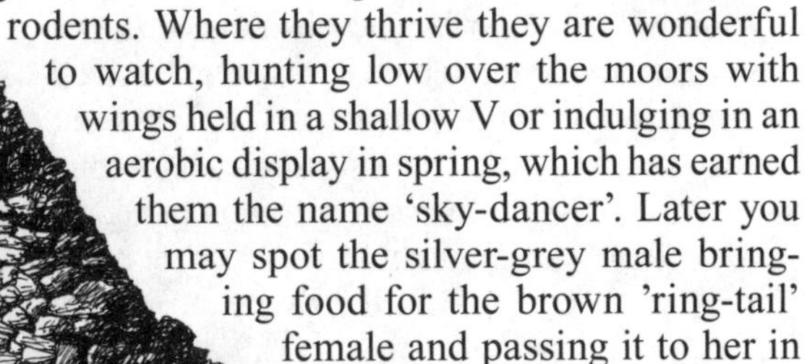

Cairn Table

John Loudoun Macadam was born in Ayr on 21st September, 1756, son of James Macadam and Susanna

Cochrane, niece to 7th Earl of Dundonald. He lived for a time in the USA until the War of Independence, when he came back to Ayr. He bought the Tar Company from Lord Dundonald in 1790. He experimented in different building materials. The tar his works produced was mainly used for weather proofing.

1 Walk out of the far end of the car park and keep left at a path junction, following a blue arrow. Go up past a small plantation of deciduous trees and cross a fence at a stile, where there is a notice about nesting hen harriers. The path winds in and out through the hummocks of old quarry workings. There are posts at frequent intervals to mark the way, some with faded red arrows. Beyond a narrow pool, on the left, the way is edged with a fence and a broken wall and begins to climb, very gently at first, across the moorland. There are sections of duck boarding across the many wet patches, where bog asphodel flowers. Look out for hen harriers quartering the moor in spring and summer.

2 Go through a kissing gate and carry on up. Eventually the old wall stops but the fence continues and the path goes up beside it, getting gradually steeper as you climb onto the ridge called The Steel. Keep on up, choosing the best way where the well-used path braids, until you come to a cross of paths. Turn left or keep straight on, either will do, they meet again on the summit ridge. A short walk along the broad path on the summit ridge brings you to a magnificent pointed cairn, built as a war memorial. There is also a trig point on the rocky summit, a view indicator and a little further on, a huge heap of stones, which is probably a Bronze Age burial cairn. The view from Cairn Table, 1944 ft/593m, is spectacular, of Arran, the western Southern Uplands, and as far north as Ben Lomond.

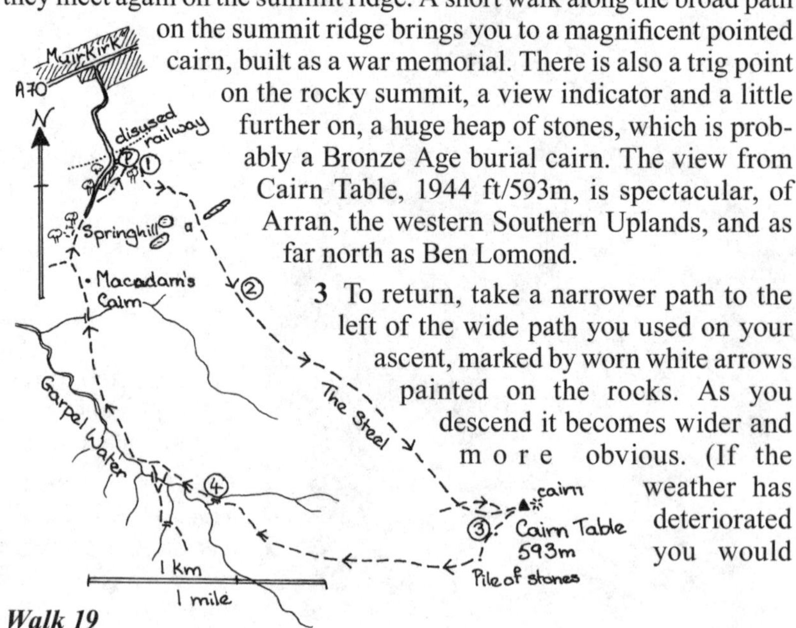

3 To return, take a narrower path to the left of the wide path you used on your ascent, marked by worn white arrows painted on the rocks. As you descend it becomes wider and more obvious. (If the weather has deteriorated you would

Walk 19

be wiser to return by your upward route.) Carry on down a short steep rocky section and then along the distinct path running south-west with apparently limitless hills spreading out ahead. Follow the path as it swings right to run along the top of a ridge, which drops down towards the valley of the Garpel Water. Lower down the way divides, with an ATV track going ahead and the footpath proper heading right. Keep to the footpath, which can be wet, and go down to cross a tributary burn on a good footbridge.

4 Contour the hillside beyond, then come down steps to join a substantial track, which you climb. Keep right and follow the track down the valley. As it moves away from the river, look for red grouse in the heather on either side. Go past a cairn, a memorial to John Macadam of tarmac fame. Ignore a waymarked path on your left. Walk on past a copse of deciduous trees, to the site of Springhill House where John Macadam once lived. Go though a gate and look for a waymarked path on the right running round behind houses. Follow this back to the car park.

Hen harrier (female)

Practicals

Type of walk: *This is an easy pleasant climb, with well-used paths and good gates, bridges, and duck-boarding across many of the wetter areas. The moor can be very wet and in some places you will have to pick your way carefully. The views are splendid.*

Distance: 6 miles/9.5km
Time: 3–4 hours
Maps: OS Explorer 328/Landranger 71

Walk 20

Douglas and Douglas Water

Park in the village of Douglas, behind the ancient church of St Brides, grid ref 836310. Access this from the M74 at Junction 12 and take the A70 south-west.

The **ancient church of St Brides** existed in the 1150s and it was still in use during the 13th century. It was rebuilt in the late 13th century. Today only the chancel, the ruins of the Inglis Aisle and the clock tower remain. The church is dedicated to St Bride who was Patron Saint of the Douglas family. The church was gifted to the Ministry of Works by the Douglas and Angus Estates during the mid 1940s.

1 From the 'back' gates of St Brides, walk ahead down Kirkgate, with cottages to the right and a row of rowans to your left. There is also a children's play area on the grassy area on your left, with woodland beyond. Walk ahead past the Polish Memorial Garden and go on to take the signed right-of-way to 'Douglas Castle'. Follow the track into pastures with scattered lime trees. In a few steps, go left through a gate labelled Stable Lake and follow the

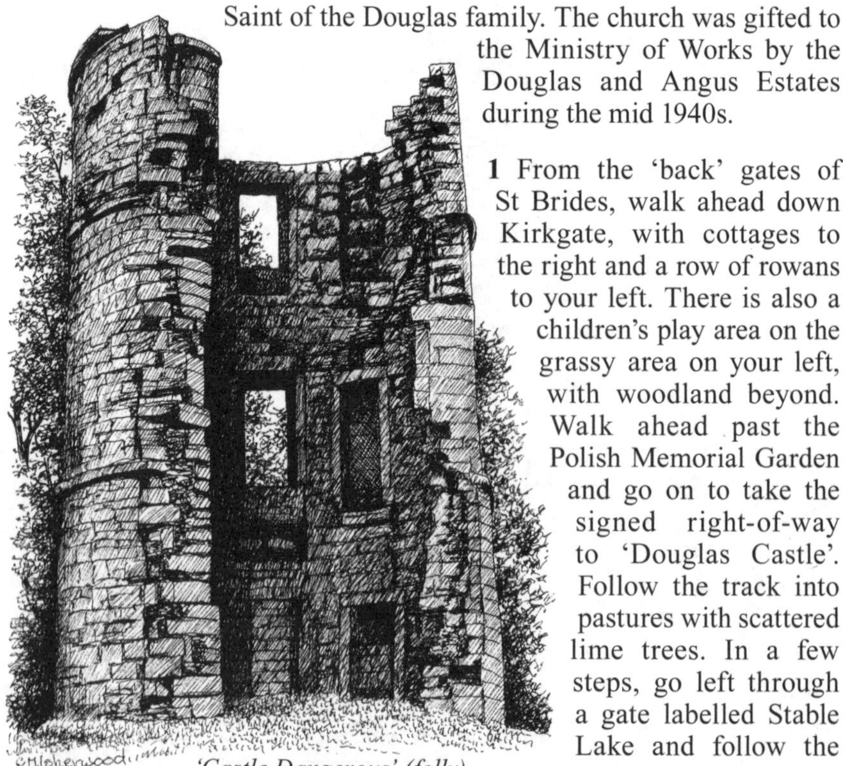

'Castle Dangerous' (folly)

path to the edge of the lake, where you might spot a peregrine and where flowering rush thrives among the reeds.

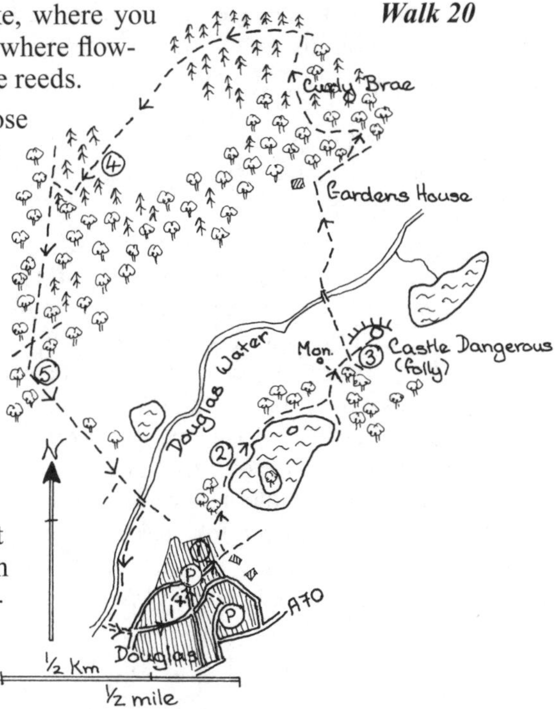

2 The lake has two islands. Close by the largest, you might spot pairs of swans marshalling large broods of cygnets. Continue beside the placid pool and then go on over the pasture, still on the narrow path, to join a track, where you turn left. Stroll on the lovely parkland of the estate that once belonged to the Douglas Home family. Away to your left is a monument erected to the Cameronian Regiment, which was disbanded at Douglas in 1968. To your right, reached by a path, stand the remains of a folly. The castle was built beyond the folly and all trace of it has gone. The folly was called 'Castle Dangerous', by Sir Walter Scott.

3 Return to the track and turn right to walk to the iron bridge, its sturdy structure reminding you that the grounds were once used by the army for training. Beyond the bridge over the Douglas Water, where sand martins fly fast after insects, follow the track to go past, on your left, Gardens House. Follow the track round right and walk on for a short way to a gated track on your left. Go through the gate and climb gently through deciduous woodland. Head on up Curly Brae to a T-junction, where you turn left into dense forest. This is soon replaced by scattered birch and open heather on either side of the good track. Marsh woundwort, sneezewort and ragged robin flower along the way and clumps of white foxgloves grow among the long grass.

4 Then the track enters more forest, which closes in on the track again. Here look for redpolls in the tree tops. A few

Redpoll

steps along the track turns right and becomes very wet. Fortunately a T-junction is soon reached and you need to turn left here. This track is mainly dry but where it is boggy look for small by-passes made by earlier walkers. At a Y-junction take the left-hand path and descend through deciduous woodland to arrive at a fence, with a large pasture beyond. Look left for a fine view of several lakes, including Stable Lake visited earlier.

5 Turn right and wind on round left, beside the fence, with the pleasing parkland stretching away beyond. Go through a wrought iron kissing gate into a large field, from where there is a fine view of the village. Descend by the fence on your left, passing through a clump of large beech trees. Go ahead along a fenced grassy path towards a blue footbridge over the Douglas Water. Wriggle through the squeeze stile to cross the bridge. Beyond, turn right to walk with the fence to your left and the burn beside you on the right. Follow the glorious path, which in summer is a colourful flower garden, and remain on it until you reach a stile. Once over, turn left on a track and walk into Douglas enjoying its fine buildings. Turn left to walk a signed ginnel to visit the church of St Bride. Leave by the 'back gate' to rejoin your car.

Flowering Rush

Practicals

Type of walk: *A fairly short delightful walk, mainly level for most of the way and with much to see as you pass through parkland, forest and along the riverbank.*

Distance:	4 miles/6.5km
Time:	2–3 hours
Maps:	OS Explorer 335/Landranger 71 or 72

Walk 21

Green Lowther and Lowther Hill

Park in a small parking area for several cars on the right of the A702, just beyond a small conifer plantation where the Southern Upland Way (SUW) is signed up the fell to the right, grid ref 928094. To get there, from junction 14 on the M74, follow the A702 south through Elvanfoot toward the Dalveen Pass. Ignore a left turn on a minor road then continue past a conifer forest on the left (east) side of the valley. Towards the end of the plantation the SUW comes in from the left to join the road. Cross a bridge, pass a large layby on the right (possible parking), go by several buildings at Overfingland and, 100yds/92m further south, the SUW is signed on the right at the parking space.

Lowther Hill (2368ft/725m) and **Green Lowther** (2399ft/732m) are the highest points in the high rolling moorland west of the M74. Although disfigured by radar installations and a service road between them, they still provide splendid views over the surrounding countryside. The villages of Wanlockhead and Leadhills to the north are famous for past gold and lead mining.

This is the only walk in this book where use can be made of the **SUW** and even here it runs along the boundary with Dumfries and Galloway. It is a long-distance footpath crossing much of the Border region.

Dalveen Pass

Walk 21

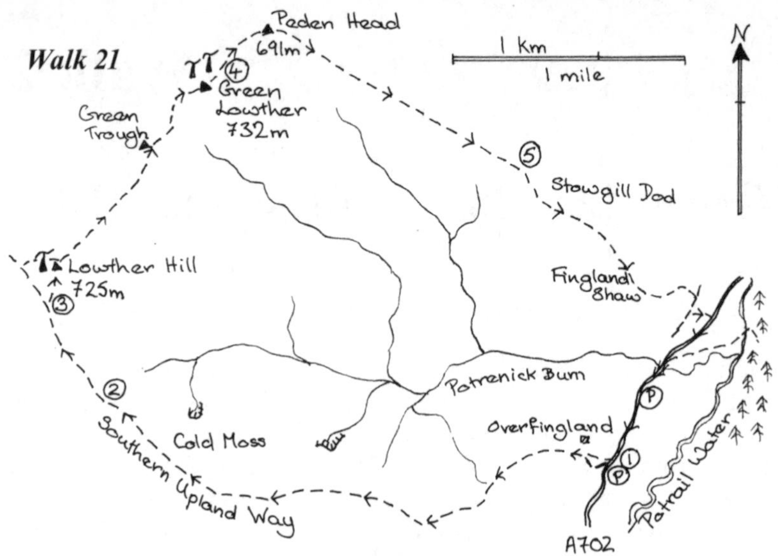

1 From the parking space, walk back towards the buildings and turn left at the SUW signpost, heading up the hill on a grassy path and through the gate by the conifer plantation. Follow the left edge of the plantation, then a wall, uphill to reach a stile. Cross and bear left along the narrow path, marked with SUW marker posts, following the old wall and newer fence as it climbs up Laght Hill to gain the ridge. From here, your route can be seen laid out on your right, following the rolling skyline above a patchwork of heather moorland and rough grass. The area is managed for red grouse, and you will doubtless hear them call at regular intervals. You may also see and hear skylarks in spring and summer.

2 Press on the SUW as it drops steeply to a deep col, with fine views down the dramatic Dalveen Pass on your left. Then ascend steeply over Comb Head, and continue on the marked path over the gentler hump of Cold Moss. From here the trail zig-zags several times to your right, leaving and returning to the fence line. Keep to the trail, following the zig-zags, until the bizarre bubble of Lowther Hill radar station looms surreally ahead.

3 As you approach the radar station, cross a stile on the left and follow the SUW underneath the station, then leave it to bear right up a grassy trod before you reach a small outbuilding. Cross a dilapidated fence to join and follow the station fence line right, east, under the bubble to reach the incongruous metalled service road. Turn right on this across the cattle grid, then left to head gently downhill away from the radar station. Follow this road northeast, past the aerials and mushrooms of Green Trough, with fine views north over the rolling lower fells. The road then curves up and left to the trig point on the summit of Green Lowther, the highest point on the ridge, itself dwarfed by a radio mast. Ravens hanging on the wind add to the rather otherworldly atmosphere.

4 Continue past the last radio mast and head downhill with the fence line on your right, through the vivid mossy green turf that gives Green Lowther its name. Cross a marshy col and head along the fence over Peden Head. Shortly after the summit, cross the fence at a junction and head right to follow the new fence line southeast along the gradually descending ridge towards Stowgill Dod. Pick your way through an area of peat hags sprinkled with *Cladonia* lichens, and follow the fence as it rises to another junction.

5 At the fence fork, go through a gate and head straight on up the rising grassy track, passing the top of Stowgill Dod on the right. Descend the broad ridge, over the final 'lump' of Fingland Shaw, and follow the track as it drops steeply and left. Watch out for hen harriers quartering the ground. After the steepest section, bear right on a green track leading across the nose of the ridge along the edge of a bracken patch. When convenient, descend left off this slope to cross a fence at a wooden gate to reach the road. Turn right, and head along the road for ½ mile/1 km past the alternative parking layby, Overfingland and Trossloss Cottage, to return to the parking spot. Be careful of fast moving traffic and heavy goods vehicles whilst you are walking along the road for ½ mile/1km.

Raven

Practicals

Type of walk: *The circuit of Lowther Hill and Green Lowther provides an enjoyable longer walk, with good views. The ascent follows the well-marked SUW, and is steep in places. The summit ridge now has a surfaced road running its length from Lowther Hill to Green Lowther, which rather spoils the 'wild' experience, but the radar stations are quite surreal and interesting in themselves. The descent line follows a fence, making navigation easier, and avoids passing through the local farms.*

Distance: 9 miles/14.5km
Time: 5–6 hours
Maps: OS Explorer 329/Landranger 78

Walk 22

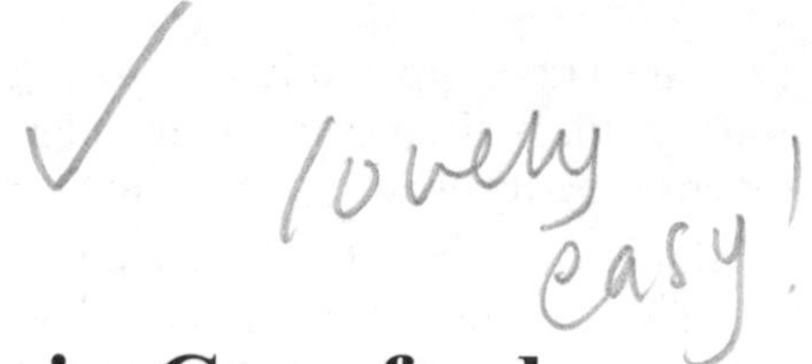

Camps Reservoir, Crawford

Park at grid ref 992224. To access this leave Crawford by a minor road, signed for the reservoir. Cross the River Clyde and drive on for about 4 miles/6.5km, turning left at a junction after the first half mile. When the dam comes into sight, you very soon reach a Y-junction. Take the right branch and park on the grass verge a short way along.

At the start of the walk around the delightful **Camps Reservoir** you pass above several houses hidden among the trees. Just before the parking area stands a fine water treatment works again easily passed as it is well landscaped with more trees. The reservoir itself snuggles deep in the hills with an isolated farm at the end of its northern limb and one bungalow at the head of the eastern limb and a farm further up the valley.

The reservoir was constructed at the end of the **1914-18 war**. Materials used were transported to the site by a branch line from Crawford. Two hundred prisoners of war helped with the construction and were accommodated on the site and paid standard wages.

Camps Reservoir

1 Walk on along the road from the parking area for a few steps to reach a cattle grid and then a gate across the road. If the latter is locked go over the fence beside it. Keep ahead along the track with deciduous and then coniferous woodland to your right and down below, left, a large grassy area and several houses beyond, among trees. Ignore a right turn and carry on past the dam, to walk the good track with the water beside you on your left. Enjoy the fine hills to your right, sloping gently downwards almost to the edge of the path. Go past an area of heather moorland that comes right down to the track. Pass a fishing hut where swallows nest under the eaves.

Grains
Martin Cleuch
Fall Cleuch Wood
Camps Knowe Wood
Camps Water
Camps Reservoir
Kneesend Wood
Campshead
½ km
½ mile

Walk 22

2 After nearly 2 miles/3.4km you wind left to cross a culvert, with an isolated bungalow to your right and grassy hills stretching away behind it. Wind round left with the track and stroll along the lovely way passing open Scots pine and then a small birch woodland. Keep your binoculars at the ready because here you might spot a pair of ospreys high up above the trees 'seeing off' an irritating buzzard. Here too you might see several oystercatchers, calling noisily from a pebbley reach of the shore. Wind on round with the path, where wild thyme borders the verge. Eventually you arrive at the end of a northern limb of the reservoir. Pass in front of a stone-built house, with sheep wandering over the grass. Behind it lonely hills slope upwards. Scattered around the sward are small bushes and in one of the few trees you might see a cuckoo surveying the landscape for the nest of an unlucky small bird.

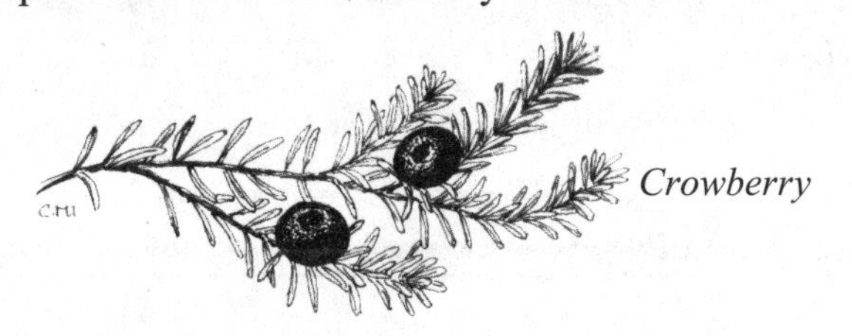

Crowberry

3 Cross another culvert and follow the track as it winds round left and begins to ascend below Fall Cleugh Wood, the only climb on this level walk and from where there is an extensive view over the reservoir. In the deciduous trees at the edge of the wood you might spot long tailed tits. In summer the track is lined with meadow sweet and rosebay willow herb. Then descend towards the dam, which you cross, pausing as you go to look east across the generally calm water. Turn right and retrace your outward steps to the parking area.

Osprey

Practicals

Type of walk: *A very pleasing stroll, with much bird life. A good walk for when the mist is low on the hills, though the views are better when it isn't.*

Distance:	6 miles/9.8km
Time:	3 hours
Maps:	OS Explorers 329 and 330/Landranger 72

Walk 23

Culter Fell

Park in a layby, on the right, immediately before the road forks after Culter Allers Farm, grid ref 031313. Access this from junction 13 of the M74 to take the A702 heading north-east to Biggar. Pass through Lamington, and in Coulter go over the bridge and turn immediately right at a sharp left-hand bend. Follow the minor road for 1 ¾ miles/3km until it drops back down into the valley bottom, pass Culter Allers Farm on your left and park in the layby which lies just beyond it. Some additional parking is available after the left-hand bend in the left branch of the road ahead; please park courteously. No vehicles are permitted further up the road. Walkers are welcomed unless shooting is in progress (look out for signs), but it is requested that larger parties (over four) seek prior permission by ringing Biggar 204010. Dogs should be on leads at all times.

Culter Fell, at **2433ft/748m**, is the highest of the sprawling, rounded group of fells between the upper reaches of the Clyde and Tweed valleys. It looks across the Clyde to Tinto. There is an old saying 'between Tintock Tap and Culter Fell, but scarce three handbreadths and an ell' (an ell was about 37 inches, and Tintock Tap is an old name for Tinto) reflecting the belief that they were the same height. However, Culter Fell is actually 133ft/41m higher.

Coulter Reservoir

Walk 23

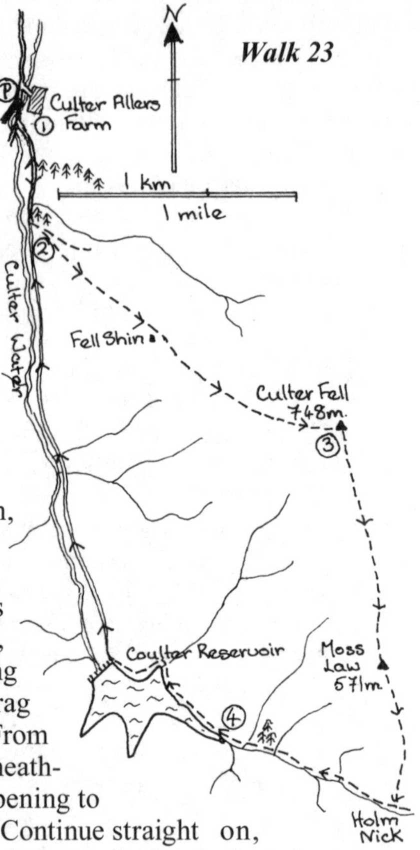

1 Take the left branch of the road, signed to Coulter Reservoir. Bend left, avoiding Birthwood straight across the bridge, and cross a cattle grid (checking for 'shooting in progress' sign if appropriate). Continue along the road with Culter Water on your right, fringed with fine beech and lime trees. Pass a conifer plantation on your left, cross Kings Beck, and turn left up a track running along the edge of a second small conifer plantation.

2 At the corner of the plantation, fork right on a grassy path leading steeply up the rounded nose of Fell Shin. Pass a series of sunken stone shooting butts, which provide convenient resting places, and turn round a small crag after which the gradient eases. From here, follow the path across the heathery shoulder and up a final steepening to the cairned ridge of Culter Fell. Continue straight on, enjoying fine views south across the watershed to the Lowther Hills and northwest to the shapely bulk of Tinto. Cross a boggy section to reach the summit trig point at a fence. There is a splendid panorama in all directions.

3 To descend, turn right and go south along a faint trod with the fence on your left and with good views over Coulter Reservoir to your right. Cross a marshy col then ascend over Moss Law, before continuing down the fence line along a more distinct track to descend into Holm Nick. Here the path meets a vehicle track coming up from the reservoir, at a convenient stone for sitting on. Turn right, following the track down the right bank of the stream, to wind through the pleasant valley. Pass a small conifer plantation on your right, cross a tributary and continue along the right bank of the stream to reach the tranquil south-east arm of Coulter Reservoir, fringed with willows. Look for dippers here.

4 Follow the well-made track along the right-hand edge of the reservoir. At the next bay, the track crosses a small stream and, looking up, you can see Culter Fell and the ridge you walked earlier. At the reservoir dam, go through an old metal gate, passing the embankment and then several buildings on your left. Continue through a white metal gate. Here the track becomes a surfaced road. Follow it past a junction coming in from the left, and continue down the pleasant valley for 1¾ miles/3km, with Culter Water on your left. Keep an eye out for birds of prey such as buzzards circling over the surrounding hillsides. Eventually you will reach the cattle grid you crossed at the start of the walk, where the road bends left and then back right to reach the car park.

Buzzard

Practicals

Type of walk: *This circuit of Culter Fell is excellent, giving fine views in all directions. The ascent of the fell is quite steep in places and there are boggy patches on the descent south but there is no technical difficulty, and no real route finding difficulty. The valley of Culter Water is particularly pleasant and tranquil.*

Distance: 8½ miles/ 13.5km
Time: 4–5 hours
Maps: OS Explorer 336/Landranger 72

Walk 24

Tinto

Park in the large car park at the northern foot of the hill grid ref 965374. To reach this, leave the A73 Abington to Lanark road to take a minor road running south at Fallburn. The car park is about 330yds/300m along this road on the left.

Tinto stands in a prominent isolated position at the northern edge of the Southern Uplands, projecting into the Midland Valley, with the Clyde winding round its feet. It is 2323ft/707m high and has a gentle conical shape. It is very obvious in views from the M74, with its conspicuous red scree below the summit. Its name may come from the Gaelic *teinnteach*, meaning fiery, because it was certainly a beacon hill. The huge cairn on the summit is traditionally said to be the site of the beacon. Nearby in the Clyde Valley are the remains of a Roman road and camps and fortlets, and there is a fine Iron Age fort at the start of the walk.

Iron Age fort, Tinto

Walk 24

1 Leave the car park by a kissing gate, beside a sign saying 'Welcome to Tinto Hill'. The path goes gently uphill along a fenced outrake. Go through another kissing gate and make a slight detour left to explore a fine ancient earthwork consisting of a series of ring dykes. In autumn look for bright red or yellow waxcap fungi in the grass. Then continue along the good reinforced path as it begins to climb across the flank of the hill. Pause at intervals to enjoy the view, and watch and listen for red grouse. In spring you may also hear skylarks and curlews.

2 The path curves round to the left and climbs up onto the ridge. There is a cairn out to the left on a spur called Totherin Hill. Join a track coming up the far side of Totherin Hill and continue upwards, now on the east side of the ridge. At a track junction take the left branch, though either will do, and climb round a rocky knoll. Carry on just below the crest of the ridge. Rejoin the path, which went round the west side of the knoll and walk up beside a fence to the summit. This is crowned with an immense cairn; climb up one of the many paths to reach the top. The trig point is off to one side, beyond a fence, but the cairn is higher. It looks like an ancient burial cairn, probably Bronze Age although there is no structure visible.

3 Because of its position on the northern flank of the southern uplands Tinto commands a

Red Grouse

Skylark

fantastic view over the Clyde Valley and to points north. Enjoy this before you begin the descent. When you reach the division of paths, about 330yds/300m below the summit, take the left path and go round the other side of the knoll above a deep cleft called Maurice's Cleuch. Then rejoin your upward path and make your way back down to the car park, with splendid views in front of you as you descend. There is a tearoom by the road junction at Fallburn which may be very welcome though it is not open all year round.

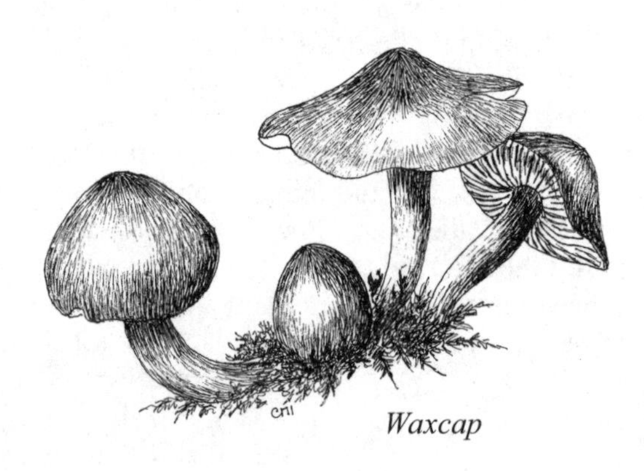

Waxcap

Practicals

Type of walk: *A very enjoyable and straightforward climb on good clear paths and tracks, and with superb views.*

Distance: 5 miles/8km
Time: 3–4 hours
Maps: Os Explorer 335/ Landranger 72

Walk 25

New Lanark and the Falls of Clyde

Park in the large car park high above New Lanark, grid ref 882427. Access this from the A73 in Lanark by the well-signed road leading south.

Robert Owen's name will always be associated with New Lanark. Two hundred years ago, as he stood above the village, he declared: "Of all the places I have yet seen I should prefer this in which to try an experiment I have long contemplated and have wished to have an opportunity to put into practice." The experiment was to turn his dreams of social reform into reality.

New Lanark

As you descend from the car park you have a first view of the lovely village, nestling in a tree-girt hollow, and standing beside the **River Clyde**. This was the village, where Robert Owen tried out his great experiment. He constructed several great cotton mills powered by the mighty Clyde and, at the same time, hoped to create an idealistic community of workers. Today New Lanark is an official UN World Heritage Site.

After exploring the delightful village, set off along the path to see Corra Linn and Bonnington Linn. These two superb waterfalls have inspired **artists and writers** since the late 1700s, including Samuel Taylor Coleridge and Sir Walter Scott. William Wordsworth described Corra Linn as "The Clyde's most majestic daughter". In 1840 JMW Turner painted, on canvas, the thundering Corra Linn. Today much of the water goes into the hydro-electric scheme so the waterfalls are only at their best on 'waterfall days' when the sluices are closed.

1 From the far end of the car park, descend the road to the village and turn left to dawdle along the street. Enjoy the fine restored buildings and Robert Owen's house. Go on down right to cross the fast-flowing mill leat and turn left. Carry on at this level then pause to look at the huge water wheel. Where the road ends go on along a path, following the signs for the 'Clyde Walkway' (CW). Go through an arch in a wall and ascend steps into woodland, the beginning of the Scottish Wildlife Trust nature reserve. After 150 yds/140m bear right on a boardwalk. Go past a weir that directs some of the river water into the leat, and where a dipper bobs up and down on a rock. Carry on for 550yds/500m beside the glorious river. Look for kingfishers on this quiet stretch. At the end of the boardwalk, go ahead. Continue on a surfaced road to pass a cottage and then Bonnington Power Station, mostly hidden by shrubs and forest trees. At the signpost bear right and climb fairly steeply into fine deciduous woodland, which in summer almost hides the great pipes that bring down water from high above to the station.

2 Soon the path levels and comes to a fine viewpoint and an interesting plaque. Sit on the seat to see the dramatic Corra Linn where, in a beautiful tree-lined basin, twin waterfalls, each 33ft/10m high, descend in a deafening roar. Then stroll on, up through pines, where the views of the waterfall are even better. Continue high above the gorge, following the signs for 'Bonnington Linn'. From March to June, peregrines nest on a bare rock on the opposite side of the gorge and there are facilities for viewing them (fee).

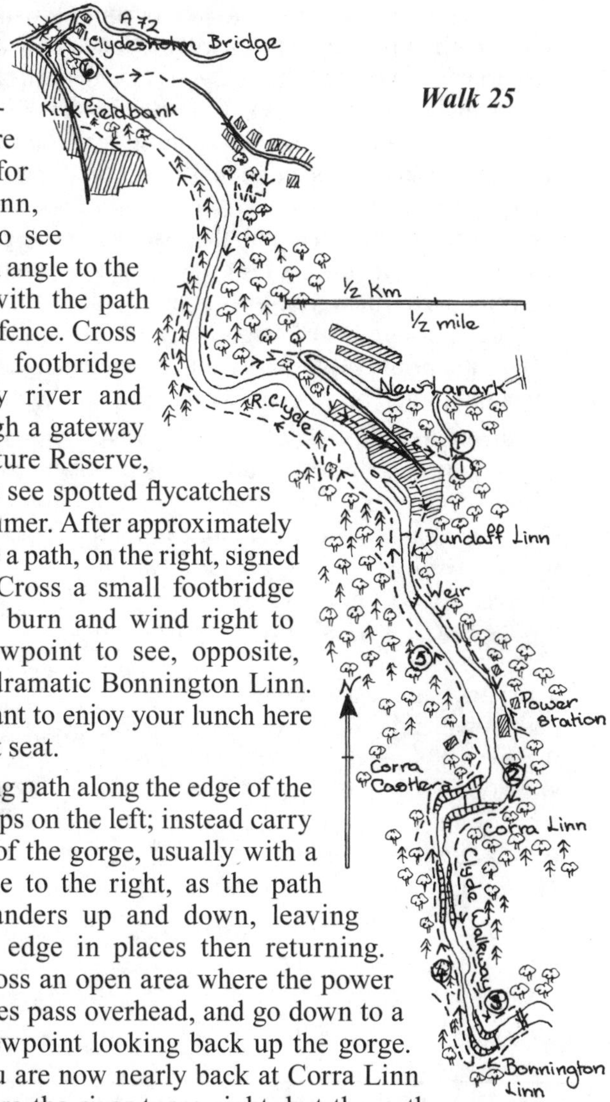

3 Press on above the river where it begins to swing left. At a right-angled bend there is a viewpoint for Bonnington Linn, slightly harder to see because it is at an angle to the path. Turn left with the path and descend to a fence. Cross the replacement footbridge over the mighty river and walk right through a gateway back into the Nature Reserve, where you might see spotted flycatchers in spring and summer. After approximately 135yds/150m take a path, on the right, signed to a viewpoint. Cross a small footbridge over a tributary burn and wind right to the splendid viewpoint to see, opposite, once again, the dramatic Bonnington Linn. Perhaps you'll want to enjoy your lunch here on the convenient seat.

4 Carry on the rising path along the edge of the ravine. Ignore steps on the left; instead carry on along the lip of the gorge, usually with a fence to the right, as the path meanders up and down, leaving the edge in places then returning. Cross an open area where the power lines pass overhead, and go down to a viewpoint looking back up the gorge. You are now nearly back at Corra Linn where the river turns right, but the path goes left and joins an upper path. Bear right and wind round with fields to the left and the ruins of Corra Castle on the right. This was a tower house built by the Bannatyne family. The path goes down quite steeply with three viewpoints for the waterfall, although in this case the view is better from the other side of the river.

Peregrine

5 The path continues to rise and fall, becoming wider. Ignore a junction with a path to the left. The power station is now behind you and soon New Lanark comes into view opposite, although it is quite hard to get a good view through the trees. When level with the far end of the village the path rises and swings left, coming up to a track, where you turn right. It runs along the edge of a forest, with pastures on the left, and then goes back into the trees. Soon houses appear above on the left and the path swings round to join the road in Kirkfieldbank. Turn right and walk down the road to its lowest point where you turn right to cross the old bridge over the river. This is the Clyde Walkway again and a sign before the bridge instructs you to turn right through the gate at the far side of the bridge. It looks like a garden gate but actually leads down a metalled track between two cottages, then ends at a field gate.

6 Go through and walk a pleasant grassy way along the riverbank. Beyond the next gate the path climbs steeply up steps round a Scottish Water installation, then bends right at the top and becomes a road. Carry on along it through houses, climbing steadily. The road winds left, then almost immediately take a right turn (signed CW) into a park through imposing gateposts and along an avenue of limes. Then go right at the next signpost and follow the zigzag path down and down to run along above the river. It goes down steps to the bank, and soon up lots of steps again, avoiding a cliff on the riverside, to a viewpoint over New Lanark. Continue up, now on zigzags again, to join a road. Turn right to return to the path to the car park.

Lime

Practicals

Type of walk: *Good paths all the way. Quite a lot of ups and down. Much of interest. Save time to explore New Lanark.*

Distance: 7 miles/11.5km
Time: 3–4 hours
Maps: OS Explorer 335/Landranger 71 or 72

Walk 26

Strathaven, Sandford and Spectacle E'e Falls.

Park in the short stay car park, grid ref 702445, in the middle of Strathaven.

Access this by heading west on the A71 from Junction 8 on the M74. The car park is signed to the right after you go past the castle.

Save some time to visit bustling **Strathaven**, a delightful town through which flows the Powmillon Burn. Enjoy the walk around the remains of its imposing castle beside which the burn races. The Avon Water, after which the town is named, keeps well to the south-east of the town. On this walk the river is crossed by a long wooden bridge and then the way continues up beside the Kype Water, which descends in splendid falls and cataracts hurrying to join the Avon.

Legend has it that one of the **Lords of Strathaven** punished his wife, while she was still alive, by creating a niche in the castle

Strathaven Castle

wall and bricking her up inside. When part of the castle walls collapsed human remains were found.

Only ruins remain of the mill where an incident occurred which gave the falls beside it their unusual name, **Spectacle E'e (eye) falls**. The story goes that an unsuitable lad fell in love with the beautiful daughter of the miller who put an end to the romance. In revenge the lad put his spectacles in the thatch of the roof of the mill. When the sun shone the thatch caught fire and the mill burned to the ground.

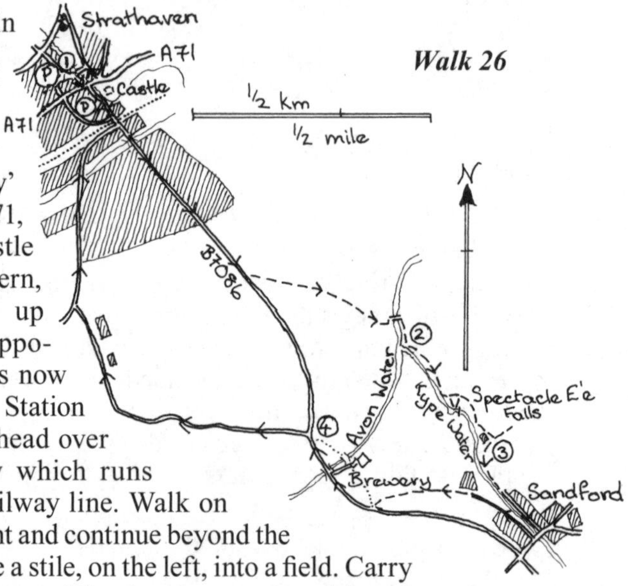

Walk 26

1 Return to the main street, turn right, and a short way along cross diagonally to walk up a narrow 'no entry' ginnel. At the A71, close to the Castle and the Castle Tavern, cross and walk up Todshill Street opposite. The Castle is now on your left. Join Station Road and walk ahead over the bridge below which runs an old disused railway line. Walk on along the pavement and continue beyond the houses. Soon, take a stile, on the left, into a field. Carry on down beside a row of fine beeches to your right, where you might spot a flock of siskin. Go through the stile and on down, enjoying the pleasing views over the delectable countryside, towards the long wooden bridge over the Avon Water. Beyond turn right and follow the path as it winds left beside the Kype Water.

2 Walk the narrow mainly well-reinforced path and then climb railed wooden steps. At the first 'landing' turn right to walk through the ruins of the mill and on along the wooden viewpoint from where you have a great view of the magnificent falls. If the river is in spate you might get caught in the spray. Return to the path and go on up more railed steps. Beyond continue on the way that winds round right, high above the burn, where you might like to sit on a seat and enjoy more of the impetuous burn. Carry on across a gated footbridge and then over a field with trees to the right to climb a stile onto a narrow lane.

3 Bear right and walk on to pass Tweedie Mill and continue to a T-junction in the village of Sandford. Go right across the road bridge over the Kype Water and then, immediately, stroll right down the 'Private' road. This soon becomes a rough track and drops down to join the B7086. Curve round right with the pavement. Look down right see the Strathaven Brewery and a picturesque old bridge.

4 Carry on until opposite a left turn. Cross the busy road, with care, and walk up the quiet lane, where in autumn and winter you might spot a large flock of bramblings feasting on mast, their most favoured food, from one of the large beech trees. Follow the lane as it winds right and continues to a wider road. Turn right to walk down through the houses. Walk left at the road you took to Sandford, cross the old railway bridge and walk straight ahead to the centre of Strathaven and then the car park.

Bramblings

Practicals

Type of walk: *Starts and ends at a delightful town. Takes you through pleasing countryside on paths, tracks and narrow lanes. Some road walking. Visits a spectacular waterfall.*

Distance: 3 miles/5km
Time: 1–2 hours.
Maps: OS Explorer 335/Landranger 71

Walk 27

Loudoun Hill

Park in Darvel, in the large car park on the left of Ranoldcoup Road, grid ref 564373. To reach this turn south off the A71 (Main Street), just east of Hastings Square.

Loudoun Hill is a spectacular **volcanic plug**; the lava solidified in the central crater of the volcano and then the outer part eroded away over thousands of years to leave this steep-sided hill.

Alexander Fleming who discovered penicillin was born near Darvel in 1881. There are a monument and a bust commemorating him in Hastings Square. At the opposite side of the square is the Dagon Stone, a curiously shaped stone dating from the Bronze Age.

The **Long Cairn** is 335ft/110m in length and said to be the longest in Scotland. It is around 5,000 years old, and although it has been mined for much of its stone, it still shows the hollows, which were the five burial chambers.

The whole of the Irvine Valley, originally settled in the 16th

'Spirit of Scotland' sculpture and Loudoun Hill

century by Flemish weavers, was an important textile centre exporting high quality cotton lace. **Darvel** was established in 1752 by the 4th Earl of Loudoun to provide housing and employment for displaced farm workers. The weaving industry flourished and especially lace making. The mills are now demolished.

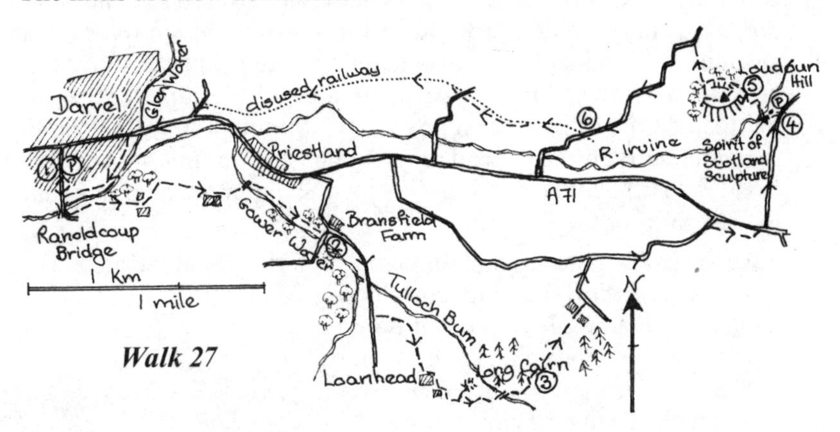

Walk 27

1 From the car park, carry on down Ranoldcoup Road and cross the bridge over the River Irvine. Wind left with the road and where it turns right carry straight on following the sign for Long Cairn Walk, to climb a narrow metalled way with woods to the left and open pasture to the right. At the top of the hill the road becomes a track. Go past two houses and through a gate to wind left by the second house and walk down the field, swinging right to High Greenbank Farm. Go on past the farm and down its track to cross Slacks Bridge, an attractive packhorse bridge with almost no parapet, over the Gower Water. At the far side go down steps to walk a narrow path through the woodland belt beside the burn. In spring this is full of wood anemones, celandines and primroses and later, bluebells. At the far end of the trees, go up steps to turn left along a minor road to Bransfield Farm.

2 Turn right up another narrow road in front of the farm. Cross the Tulloch Burn, a tributary of the Gower Water, and before the road starts to climb seriously uphill take a signed road on the left for Loanhead Farm. Continue on the track to pass to the left of the farm and wind left then right round its outbuildings. Walk on down the edge of the field, go through a gate and continue straight ahead, with a detour round a pool in the path after heavy rain. At the fence end go left through a gate to visit the Long Cairn on its narrow spur projecting above the Tulloch Burn. Then return to the path and turn left along a fenced strip. Go through a gate and wind uphill below mature beech trees to descend gently to a bridge over the Tulloch Burn. Cross and climb round on the path from the old ford to reach a cross of paths at the top of the hill.

3 Go straight ahead through a gate and follow the slightly raised track along the edge of two fields to pass between two cottages and walk on down to a minor road. Turn left and walk below beech trees towards splendid Loudoun Hill. At a T-junction turn right and carry on down to cross an old railway line. As you approach the A71 look for the signed old road on the right. Take it and follow it through new tree plantings to come out onto the A-road almost opposite a minor signed road to Loudoun Hill and the Spirit of Scotland Sculpture. Go up this road to the car park for the sculpture.

4 Take the gate on the left and immediately fork right along a good path. Poppies, cornflowers, and corn marigolds have been planted here. Go on down to a picnic table, an excellent spot to stop and enjoy the view whilst you eat your lunch. Then carry on down to admire the sculpture with Loudoun Hill behind. Make your way down the grassy path to cross a stile, then a bridge over the infant River Irvine. Zigzag up the steep bank at the far side to reach a terrace below the cliffs of Loudoun Hill. Wind round to the right of the hill and climb steeply up a pasture and round a fence corner into woodland. A rather muddy path runs through the trees. If you want to climb the hill keep taking left turns and eventually zigzag up through the trees and out onto steep grassy slopes. In some places some easy scrambling is necessary. Soon, however, you emerge onto the top of the hill just below the trig point. Enjoy the splendid view.

5 Retrace your steps, or walk west to the end of the summit where you will find another steep well-used grassy path leading down. There are a couple of rock steps which are slippery in wet weather but with care you soon arrive down in the beech wood again. Turn right

Corn marigold and Cornflower

along a path which runs round the base of the hill. (If you do not fancy the steep climb up and down again, you can just contour round the base on this path). Go left where there is a way through the fence. Cross a field to a stile, then another to come out on a road. Turn left and follow the many twists downhill.

6 The road passes between the pillars of an old railway viaduct. Just before this take the right turn and cross the wall on your left where there is a step and a post to help you. Climb the slanted, stepped way up the embankment. The railway track leads all the way back to Darvel, although soon after the start follow a signed path up the embankment to cross stiles at the top and go along above the line for a while. Beyond the next bridge the path goes back down to the track. There is also a very wet place where you have to go left up the embankment and then later down off the side to avoid a bridgeless gap. Look for fieldfares in autumn, feasting on the berries which line the track. Go past a seat and over a stile, then another, to reach a road. Turn left and go downhill to the A71. Cross with care and walk along the pavement into Darvel. Go over the bridge across the Glen Water and almost immediately turn left down a path which runs beside the river, now joined with the Irvine. This is lovely with mature trees overhanging the turbulent water. At Ranoldcoup Road turn right to return to the car park.

Fieldfare

Practicals

Type of walk: *A varied and interesting walk, mostly well-signed. Some road walking. The climb up Loudoun Hill is steep and rocky in places but well worth it for the view. However if you do not wish to go up it is easily by-passed; just carry on through the wood along its base.*

Distance: 9 miles/14.5km
Time: 5 hours
Maps: OS Explorer 334/Landranger 71

Walk 28

Dean Castle Country Park, Kilmarnock

Park at the Visitor Centre, grid ref 437393, which stands at the end of a long tree-lined drive. Access this from the south by leaving the A77 at Bellfield Interchange and follow signs through Kilmarnock. From the B7038, Glasgow Road, turn right into Dean Road. Turn left into the Park entrance as directed, before you reach the river. The car park is on the right. From the north, leave the A77 on the B7082 and turn right into Dean Road. Go onto cross the bridge over Kilmarnock Water and the entrance is along on the right.

Dean Castle Country Park is another of Ayrshire's wonderful estates that has been gifted to the people of a nearby large town. These Parks generally provide activities for all ages, including some lovely walks. Entry to the park and the castle is free.

Dean Castle

The Castle was built on lands given to the **Boyd family by Robert the Bruce**. It takes its name from 'The Dean' or wooded valley. The Keep dates from around 1350 and the Palace was added about 1470. The family lived at the castle for 400 years. In 1899 the 8th Lord Howard de Walden inherited the castle. He died in 1946 and his heir, his son, gifted the castle and estate to the people of Kilmarnock. In 1976 the castle was opened to the public.

1 From the parking area walk right with the Visitor Centre to your left. Carry on to pass to the right of the castle. Cross the bridge over the hurrying Fenwick Water and turn left to walk up beside it through fine woodland. At the next bridge walk half way across to enjoy the view up and down the tree-lined river. Then return to the path, cross the road and follow the waymarked, reinforced path that leaves the riverside and climbs steadily up through more glorious woodland. Pass a large house to the left, Dean Castle riding school, with several horses in the fenced field beside you.

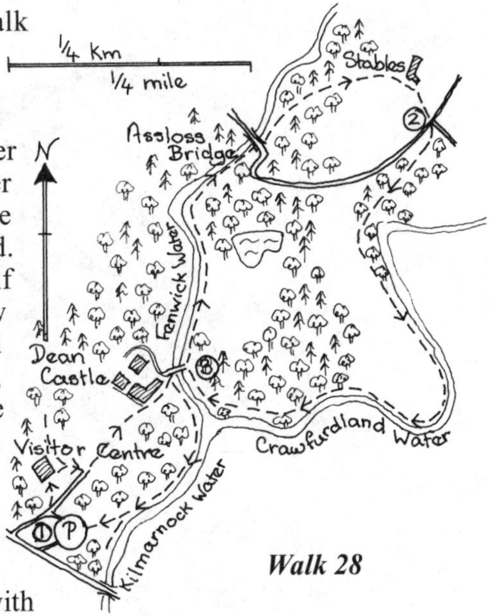

Walk 28

2 Cross Assloss Road, a road through the Park. Go through a gateway opposite and turn right to wind on along a good track through beech woodland. You can now look down on the Craufurdland Water far below where notice should be taken of the warning signs. The path then descends gently to come beside the lovely tumbling water once more. There are now fields on the right. Go on along the curving path as it eventually begins to move away from the river into more superb woodland.

3 Turn left to see the castle straight head. Cross, once again, the bridge over the Fenwick Water and take the next left turn to walk beside the surging river as it joins the Craufurdland Water to become the Kilmarnock Water. Wind round with the latter through splendid forest trees. Watch out for where a track climbs steeply uphill through mixed woodland where you might spot a tree creeper assiduously searching the tree bark for food. Listen for the sweet song of a wren as you continue to the parking area, close to the Visitor Centre once more.

Wren

Practicals

Type of Walk: *Short and quite delightful, particularly in the autumn when the woodlands are a riot of colour.*

Distance: 2 miles/3.4km
Time: 1–2 hours
Maps: OS Explorer 333/Landranger 70

Walk 29

Eglinton Country Park, Kilwinning

Park at the Visitor Centre car park, grid ref 319418. Access this from the A78 and then the B7080, north of Irvine. It is well signed.

Eglinton Country Park was developed by Irvine Development Corporation and was opened in 1986 to offer visitors access to an extensive area of countryside. There is a very good network of footpaths and trails throughout the Park.

The Park is located in the grounds of the old **Eglinton Castle Estate** on the outskirts of Kilwinning. The iconic feature is the ruined castle, once home to the Eglinton family and later the Montgomeries. The first part of the walk takes you up **Belvedere Hill** to a classical folly. From here paths, through young woodland, radiate in all directions from the central hub, giving great views.

The **dramatic ruined castle** dates from 1796. It was built by the 12th Earl of Eglinton. Its roof was removed in 1925, leaving much of the shell exposed. In 1938 the ruin was used for army training and was mostly destroyed. The picturesque remains give an idea of the extent of this once majestic building.

Stones, Cairnmount Hill, Eglinton

The nearby **Tournament Bridge** was constructed for the Eglinton tournament, a medieval event held in 1839. Nearly 100,000 people attended the 3-day event. Today it has been restored and is quite magnificent.

1 Turn right out of the car park and wind right to pass a 'No Entry' sign into fine woodland. Leave it, left, immediately, to join the lower end of a very wide grassy, pathless ride up Belvedere Hill and climb to the folly at the top, in view all the way. From it radiate many paths. Go on, 45 degrees right, after enjoying the views, along a continuing grassy way, with a fenced track to your left for horse riders. To the left you have glimpses of a pool and can hear wigeon whistling on the water in autumn and winter. Follow the on-going track as it continues through woodland. Where it comes close to a road carry on left until you can visit, on the right, a very fine Doocot, where once pigeons were housed to provide food for winter banquets.

2 Wind on along the track. Ignore a path going off left and then, where the main track also goes off left, continue ahead through a more open area with woodland away to the left, beyond a small burn. Follow the path as it bears left and then right steadily climbing through open countryside to reach a fine group of standing stones on the top of Cairnmount Hill. Carry on down the good track and just before reaching the road, turn sharp left at a waymark into Sourlie Wood Nature Reserve. The track takes you through lush wet woodland where alders and willows thrive. Go on along the way to leave the woodland and follow the path as it continues left and crosses the Doura Burn on a fine metal bridge. Press on through open pastures and eventually stroll right with woodland to the right and pastures to the left, where you might spot fieldfare and reed bunting. Pass through more woodland and then along beside a stubble field to join a track coming in on the left and go right.

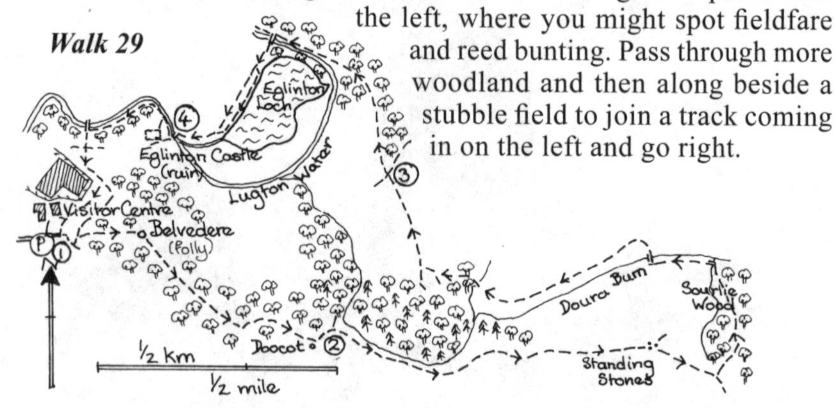

3 Stroll through more fine pastures to reach a cross of tracks. Go ahead here to continue with woodland away to the right and scattered trees to the left. Soon the way draws nearer to Eglinton Loch seen through the trees. Cross fine Chapelholme Bridge over Lugton Water and walk on along the opposite side of the loch. There are seats here and before one of them look for a narrow path that drops down to the lochshore. Turn right and follow a path through the trees and then join a boardwalk from where anglers fish. Look for tufted duck, swimming quietly in a little group. At the end of the loch climb steps to rejoin the track.

4 Continue on the track to cross Castle Bridge and a wide track. Walk ahead over the grass to view the picturesque castle ruins where you will want to have your camera ready. Then turn away north from the ruins and pass through rhododendrons to reach the track, crossed a few minutes earlier, and turn left. Walk on until you reach the splendid Tournament Bridge, perhaps using your camera again. Do not cross but turn left down a track that passes through more rhododendrons and forest trees where siskins flock. As you approach a large building site leave the path and wind round left of it. In 1958 the 17th Earl converted a building into a canning factory. The latter has been out of use for some years and it is now being redeveloped. Carry on ahead and cross a wide track to return to the parking area.

Wigeon

Practicals

Type of walk: *This is a lovely walk of contrasts on good tracks and paths but it never quite gets away from traffic noise especially if the wind is blowing from the south-west. Choose a day when the noise might be blown away in the opposite direction by a northerly wind.*

Distance: 4 ½ miles/ 7.5km
Time: 2–3 hours
Maps: OS Explorer 333/Landranger 70

Walk 30

Knock Hill Walk, Largs

Park at the beach car park at Largs, (small charge) opposite Nardini's the famous ice cream shop, grid ref 203596. If you park facing the sea you might spot goldeneye, eider, merganser, shag and cormorant.

Look for the cairn to your left just before the farm track, where a small plaque tells of **Sir Thomas Mackdougall Brisbane** who was born in the glen in 1773 and died in 1860 in Largs where he and his family had been great benefactors. His family owned the estate over which you are walking. He was Governor General of Australia's New South Wales from 1821-1826 and gave his name to the Brisbane river. When you pass the cemetery on the right, point 2, look for the ornate gates on your left. These once marked the entrance to the home of the Brisbane family.

The fine track from the start of the farm track to Brisbane Mains farm and on to the summit of The Knock was used by the grand ladies who visited the summit for a **picnic, conveyed in their horse-drawn carriages**, whilst their husbands were out shooting on the Brisbane Estate.

Brisbane Mains

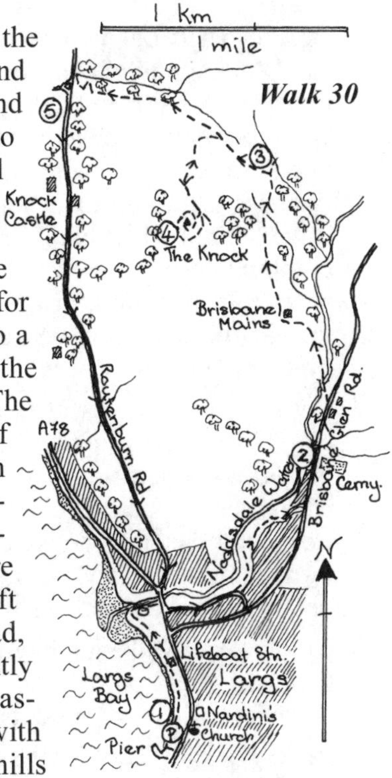

1 Walk north along the promenade, past the RNLI station. Go on until you can wind clockwise round an ornamental pond continuing with the Noddsdale Water to your left, to reach an Ayrshire Coastal Path signpost on the A78. Cross and a few steps right, bear left into Barr Crescent, lined with bungalows. Ignore a road over a bridge, then look out for the signed left turn off the road, onto a footpath bringing you close beside the burn, with bungalows to your right. The burn is overshadowed by a mixture of deciduous trees and, on its banks in late winter, snowdrops and winter heliotrope flower. Eventually this pleasing way returns you to the road where you turn left. At the T-junction walk left along Brisbane Glen Road, which takes you gently uphill into the pleasing countryside, with a fine clutch of hills and ridges to your right.

2 Carry on the quiet way, past the cemetery on the right, and stroll on until you can turn down the farm track to Brisbane Mains Farm. Pass in front of the attractive building and wind round right through a gate. Carry on through the next two gates. When you reach a sheepfold across the track, curve round right and walk beside the corrugated iron side. Beyond, ignore the gate and take the signed kissing gate beyond back onto the main track. Walk on beside beeches, curving round left to a waymarker, which directs you left on a reasonable path over a boggy field to reach the foot of a row of straggly beech.

Walk 30

1 Km
1 mile
Knock Castle
The Knock
Brisbane Mains
Routenburn Rd
A78
Noddsdale Water
Brisbane Glen Rd
Cemy.
Lifeboat Stn.
Largs
Largs Bay
Nardini's
Church
Pier

Snowdrops and Winter heliotrope

3 Go ahead here out onto the moorland on a good track which, after rain, can become quite boggy in places. Where the path divides, take the upper track but note the lower path with an orange waymark - this is your continuing track after climbing to The Knock (716ft/217m). The upper track curves gently south towards The Knock. When you reach the base of the hill bear left onto the middle of one of three paths. It becomes a wide, grassy, dry way that curls round behind the hill, climbing easily. It then winds round west and then north and round again to the summit, just like a helter-skelter. Pause by the trig point to enjoy the superb views across to Arran and Cowal and spend some time searching for traces of the ancient hill-fort.

4 Return down the spiral track and retrace your steps to the orange marker mentioned in point 3. Turn acute left to walk downhill on the good track, where you might spot a hen harrier quartering the moor, to pass through a gate. Press on downhill keeping beside a line of beech trees, and the Blackhouse Burn in its ravine, both to your right. Go through the next gate to descend quite steeply through splendid deciduous woodland to reach a narrow road, where you walk left.

5 Climb steadily along the quiet lane to pass Knock Castle on the right (private). Press on the high-level way with great views over sloping pastures to the Clyde and its islands. Stroll on to pass the golf course, where the lane begins to descend to the A78. Cross and continue ahead past the ornamental pond and wind left along the promenade to return to the car park .

Hen Harrier (male)

Practicals

Type of walk: *A very satisfactory walk to a pleasing hill. After rain the first part of the track over the moor can be boggy. The return lane is two miles long, but it is quiet and a pleasure to walk. Good views.*

Distance: 7 miles/11.5 km
Time: 4 hours
Maps: OS Explorer 341/Landranger 63

Walk 31

Fintray Bay, Great Cumbrae

Park at Fintray Bay, grid ref 159569. To access this, take the ferry from Largs to the island. Drive left and pass through Millport, the only town on the island, and continue round the coast to reach Fintray Bay. If on foot take the shuttle bus from the ferry into Millport and start your walk at Golf Road, Point 5.

Great Cumbrae has been inhabited since the last ice-age. Today it has a **population of just below 1500** (2001 census), which increases substantially during the summer tourist season. For many centuries the Marquess of Bute and the Earl of Glasgow shared ownership of the island. In 1999 the final feudal owner, Johnny Dumfries, now Bute, put the island up for sale, with first refusal given to the farmer tenants. Today the island's land is owned by farmers, the other major land owner being the Millport golf club.

The Great Cumbrae **fault line** runs north-east to south-west and has formed several interesting rock formations including Lion's Rock, Queen Victoria's face and Crocodile Rock. On the western coastline look for raised beaches. At Bell Bay, the island's highest waterfall, Horse Falls, tumbles over the old sea cliff.

Arran Hills from Fintray, Cumbrae

1 From the car park at Fintray Bay walk, south, towards Millport, using the pavement on the left of the road. To the right lies the sparkling extensive Firth of Clyde and to the left a belt of deciduous woodland shades the narrow quiet road. One hundred yards along a signposted path leads off left, climbing quite steeply through dense vegetation to a kissing gate. Beyond, go on uphill on an indistinct path that steadily improves and becomes a delightful grassy swathe as it winds, right, along the ridge in the direction of Millport. Pass through a derelict fence and go on the pleasing way, with magnificent views over to Arran. Carry on through a gate and walk on towards Upper Kirkton. Wind right just before the farm gate of the dwelling to arrive at a signpost and a kissing gate.

2 Do not pass through but descend, right, with a hedge to the left, down the pasture on a clear path, signed 'The Targets Walk, Coastal Walk to Millport'. Pass through a gate on the left and carry on down a narrow path beside an arable field, now with the hedge to your right. Wind round, left, at the foot of the crop and, half way along, take a narrow path dropping right. Continue on the narrow path to cross a rather awkward stile and follow the path, right, as it steadily descends. Curve left and walk a distinct narrow path across a flat area to a kissing gate on to the coastal road.

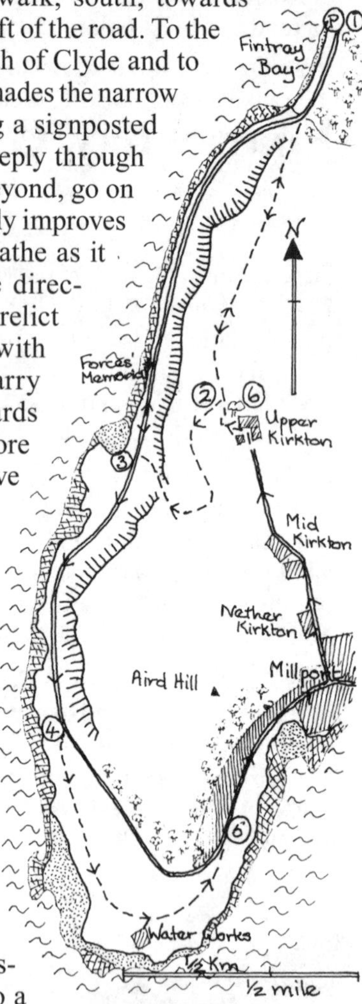

Walk 31

3 To see the fine Forces' Memorial turn right for a short way along the road and perhaps sit in the pretty garden and enjoy the view as you ponder on this solemn corner. Then walk back along the pavement to pass the entrance to the path you have just walked. Carry on past limestone cliffs on your left, where, in the spring fulmar and kittiwakes nest. Soon you reach a signpost on the opposite side of the coastal road. It directs you along a path, which keeps parallel with the road, but alas the gorse, brambles and nettles are so rampant that it soon becomes impossible to continue. Stroll on along the pavement on the left side of the road until just before you reach a small group of wooden houses.

4 Cross the road and go down a narrow path, leading towards the shore. Then take a stepped stile, tucked into the hedge on your left, to stride on left along a narrow path, just above the shore. Look for cormorants, curlew, eider and seals as you go. Enjoy this way, close to the shore, and ahead a dramatic view of Little Cumbrae and its lighthouse built in 1755. Across the Firth, look towards Arran and see if you can spot the Sleeping Warrior. Follow the path as it winds left, still close to the shore, and continues to pass through a gate. Walk on along a track beside the Scottish Water site. As the track winds towards the road, cut off right and go on towards the boatyard, where many boats are hauled up. Here the track winds left to pass through a gate and joins the Coast Road again. Cross and turn right.

Common seal

5 Carry on along the road where it winds away from the shore. Just before you reach several three-storey red sandstone houses, turn left and climb Golf Road. Go past Nether Kirkton and just beyond you might wish to visit the beautifully kept cemetery on the left, where many residents of the 19th and 20th century were buried. Go on past Mid Kirkton and wind left with the road and then left to walk a track beside the barn of Upper Kirkton. Head on along a grassy track to arrive at the kissing gate you did not take on your outward journey.

6 Pass through, wind right and then curve left, to retrace your outward route. Dawdle on along the grassy swathe with superb views ahead of the Isle of Bute. Follow the track through a gate and then on, gradually descending through the belt of trees to the Coast Road. Turn right to return to Fintray Bay.

Practicals

Type of walk: *A delight. The paths are distinct but some could be slippery after heavy rain. Some road walking. Superb views.*

Distance: 4 ¾ miles/7.5km
Time: 3 hours
Maps: OS Explorer 341/Landranger 63

Walk 32

Lunderston Bay

Park in the car park, Lunderston Bay, just off the A770 at grid ref 204746.

Lunderston Bay is the first sandy bay reached from Glasgow on the Firth of Clyde and is very popular. The views across the Firth to Dunoon and Cowal, and down to Arran are dramatic. The bay is fringed with areas of seaweed and these become more frequent as you walk south. They provide rich feeding grounds for a variety of waders. The waters offshore provide food for sea duck. Large flocks of eider congregate in late summer, sometimes up to 500, mostly males. Some distance behind the bay are sandstone cliffs, now wooded. They were once sea cliffs but have been stranded behind the wide wave cut platform, or raised beach, as the land has risen after the last glaciation. This walk skirts their base.

Lunderston Bay

1 Walk along the track that leads south out of the car park, just above the shore, with the Firth of Clyde to your right. Very soon the reinforced way ceases and a delightful path continues. Look for eiders on the water and oystercatchers grazing with sheep in the pasture to your left. Listen for wigeon whistling along the water's edge and for curlews calling as they feed in the mud. Further along you might spot redshank, turnstones, and ringed plover. The path then takes you along above a wide beach and then curves round above the shore to pass through a large area of sea buckthorn before edging Crowhill Wood.

2 A short way along, look for a path leading left, away from the shore. It soon reaches a T-junction where you turn left. The track is wide but can be very wet after rain as it moves into glorious deciduous woodland. It curves on away from the shore, almost to the side of the wood and then it winds round right still wet underfoot. It keeps near the edge of the woodland and you can glimpse the sheep feeding in the pastures seen on the way out. Eventually the track improves for a short distance and then it climbs up and becomes muddy once more.

3 At the top of the hill, turn left onto a sturdier track to pass through forestry with a dense understorey of rhododendrons. Go past a house in the trees on the left. Descend steadily to reach a bungalow on the right. Opposite, go through a gate to walk a track that takes you through sheep pasture, with a fence to the right, to a gate onto the shore path once more. Turn right along the shore path to return to the car park. As you go look across the Firth to Dunoon and as you near the car park you might wish to pause on the pleasing sands below.

Walk 32

Eiders

Practicals

Type of walk: *Short but very pleasant after a dry spell. The shore path is a delight. The way through the woods can be muddy but the woodland is very fine. Excellent walk for birdwatchers.*

Distance: 3 miles/5km
Time: 2 hours
Maps: OS Explorer 341/Landranger 63

Walk 33

Greenock Cut

Park in the large car park at Greenock Cut Visitor Centre, Cornalees, grid ref 247722. Access this from the A78, north-east of the Bankfoot roundabout, between Greenock and Inverkip, and follow a pleasing unclassified road (signposted to the Centre) over moorland and through Shielhill Glen.

The **Greenock Cut** is 4 ½ miles/7.4km long. In the 19th century the Cut carried water from Loch Thom to Greenock supplying the residents with drinking water, and water power to the woollen mills, foundries and a paper mill. It was constructed between 1825-1827 by the civil engineer Robert Thom and Loch Thom is named after him.

The walk starts from the Visitor Centre and continues beside the Compensation Reservoir and then Loch Thom before climbing over the

Bridge, Greenock Cut

open moor to descend to Overton and Waterman's Cottage. From here the water in the Cut descends in many cascades to the River Clyde.

Note the 23 small **stone bridges** that span the narrow waterway and the ruins of the two huts used by the men who cared for the Cut and kept it ice-free. In 1971 it fell out of use, superseded by a tunnel.

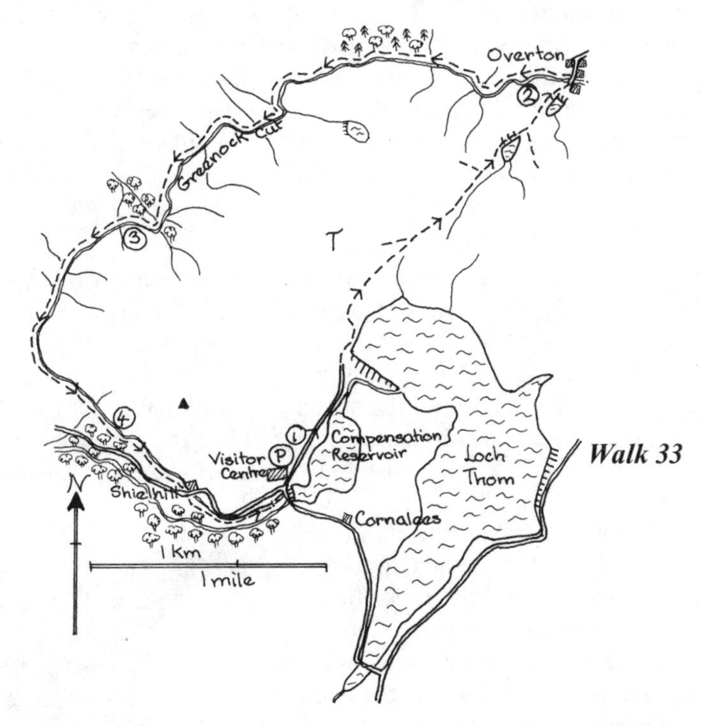

Walk 33

1 Return to the road and turn left to pass to the left of the café. Stroll on along a level tarmacked track, with moorland stretching away on the left and the Compensation Reservoir to the right. All around range misty hills. Climb gently towards Loch Thom Cottage beside the extensive Loch Thom, which is sometimes known as the Great Reservoir. Go through an iron kissing gate, where the tarmac ends, to continue on a rougher but good track to the brow of the hill, ignoring any left or right turns that lead to other small reservoirs. Here, begin your descent on the main path, with fine views across the Firth of Clyde to the Highland hills beyond. Go through another gate, close to a small reservoir, and cross the dam to wind round right at its far end. Continue on the distinct way beside a second small reservoir. Carry on downhill with views of Greenock below and the wide Firth beyond. A short way along you reach a cottage. Go through a gate to its left, and turn left to begin your walk along the well-surfaced path beside the fascinating Cut.

2 As you go enjoy the many small sturdy bridges that span the waterway, look for the fine stonework that lines the wall of the embanked path and later the natural rock face on the opposite bank. Regularly, fast flowing streams come tumbling down from the moors and, where they join the Cut, the water is controlled by sluices beside which sometimes stands a stone built shelter. Pause to enjoy the views down to Gourock and across the Firth to Dunoon, Cowal, Bute and Great Cumbrae. The brooding moors come right down to the far side of the Cut, as it contours along the side of the hills, and over these you might spot a buzzard or a sparrow hawk.

3 Stroll the path as it winds into the moorland and is often sheltered by trees and go on where it curves, quite safely, round the end of a ridge. All along the way on the far bank, grow a multitude of plants and small bushes and further along great clumps of gorse come right up to the fence. Carry on the so easy-to-walk path as it snakes below the craggy outcrops of Cauldron Hill. Then the cut turns its back on the Firth below Dunrod Hill and the views change. Pastures stretch away to the right and large areas of woodland cover the slopes and far down below. Here in the Cut look for dippers on the little rocks that project from the bed of the waterway. You might also spot an adventurous wren flitting from one side to the other of the narrow channel or a goldfinch feeding on seeds.

Dipper

4 Follow the track as it becomes shadowed by conifers, to the left, and alders to the right; these line the steep slopes down to the Kip Water that flows through Shielhill Glen. Then the trees are left behind as you approach Shielhill Farm. Cross the narrow road and go through the metal gate opposite. Stride on with the Cut beside you, left, to pass through a gate into woodland. Here steps lead down to a picnic table and along the Kelly Burn – but this walk continues along the main track from where you can look down on the burn descending in magnificent peat-stained cascades and falls. Carry on and wind steadily left with the path. Suddenly you come upon a tremendous fall (after heavy rain) as water from the reservoirs above descend the overflow in a great white curtain, plummeting into a seething plunge pool. Turn left over a lock bridge that also controls the flow of water, and then right, to reach the delightful visitor centre set in its lovely but so lonely surroundings.

Gorse

Practicals

Type of walk: *This is a delightful, very interesting walk, all on good paths. It leads you up onto to the moors, past large stretches of water and along The Cut on an excellent path with great views over the Firth of Clyde to islands beyond.*

Distance: 7½ miles/12km

Time: 3–4 hours

Maps: OS Explorer 341/Landranger 63

Walk 34

Locherwood and Ladymuir Woodland
Craig Minnan and Windy Hill

Park on the B786, 3 ½ miles/5.5km north of Lochwinnoch, grid ref 354641. The small parking area is on the west side of the road and is very easy to miss.

At the start and finish of the walk you pass through **Locherwood Community Woodland**. This was planted in the mid 1990s as a woodland with free access for local people and a haven for wild life. The trees - oak, ash, birch, beech and rowan - are still young but appear to be doing very well. In the grassy areas near the start of the walk you may find greater butterfly orchid in the late spring and early summer and also look out for small pearl-bordered fritillary butterflies.

Beyond the community woodland the walk becomes more wild and adventurous, as it continues above Renfrewshire's rolling farmland into **coniferous plantations** some of which have already been clear-felled and will have caused some of the boggy sections. All but one of the wooden bridges that cross the lively burn have rails and all of them have wire netting over the boards to prevent walkers slipping.

Windy Hill

Walk 34

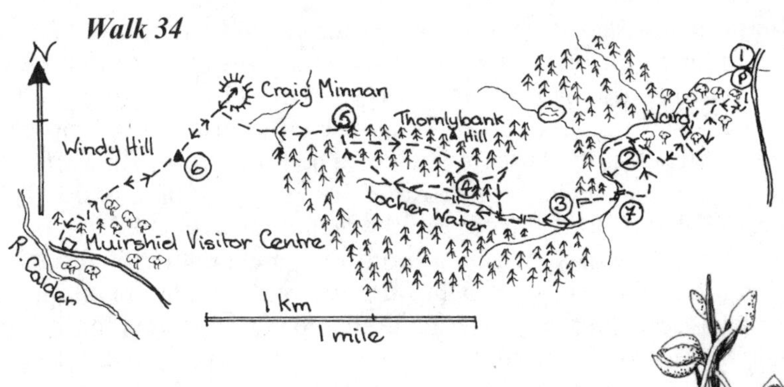

1 Walk the track leading out of the parking area, passing through immature but thriving ash and oak. Keep on the winding track, walking below several magnificent old beech until you can spot, ahead, Ward House (private) through the trees. Here take, left, a pleasing grassy trod through young ash and oak, bursting out of their plastic protective sleeves, and follow the trod as it winds right to reach a track. Bear right as directed by the colour-ringed marker post. Just before the outbuildings of the house, curve left to stroll a good track until you reach another marker post, red banded, where you go right, beside a mossy wall and tall trees shadowing you, both on the left. Ignore a signed track going off left, your return path.

2 Move out onto open moorland where you might see black grouse and, at the marker post, notice the picnic table up on the right. Here you have a choice of three paths. Take the middle one that leads you beside conifers on your left. This delightful path brings you to the side of a small burn, Locher Water. Stroll left here, with the hurrying stream to your right. Go over a little opening in the low wall ahead and carry on the pleasant way, with woodland set back on either side. Step through the gap in another little cross wall and then head right to go over a sturdy bridge above the tumbling water. Wind, right, round the edge of a conifer and then a larch plantation, to head on to the next waymark to follow the blue banded post.

CMI

Butterfly Orchid

3 Bear left as directed with a wall to your left and a vast area of clear-fell to the right. Just before a narrow craggy ravine an information board displays a map and an arrow showing where you are. Follow the narrow path round right with more conifers to the left. Ignore the next footbridge, to your left, and go on up the narrow path over open ground until you can cross a railed bridge to the other side of the burn. Walk on along the edge of the plantation and pause at a pleasant corner to look down on a footbridge and another picnic table. This is your return route later on in the walk. Continue along the bank with the burn on your right until you reach the next footbridge, which you cross. Here the burn becomes narrower and quieter.

4 Press on along the path through a ride, which soon begins to climb quite steeply to reach a rather spartan hide, used for deer and bird watching. Continue on the raised path over the large boggy grassland area, the source of the Locher Water, seen from the hide. Stroll on the way as it curves right to a footbridge, which you cross. Beyond, the way then leads you, right, into a plantation and climbs again to a forest road. Cross and walk ahead to the ladderstile onto boggy moorland, with a view of Craig Minnan and a little stretch of Windy Hill to your left.

5 Some walkers will wish to turn back from here but, for those who wish to go on, cross the ladderstile and turn left. Follow an often very damp trod running along the walled and fenced forest edge. After 980ft/300m the wall and the trod descend gently to a shallow valley at the corner of the plantation. Step over a little stream and turn left on a trod, then follow the fence line round to the right. The ground immediately beside the fence is generally very wet in places and you may wish to take to the heather on your right. Cross a larger burn and pass recent planting on your left, in the gap between Windy Hill and Craig Minnan. Continue through the heather to reach a stile at the fence junction on your left. Turn right here to ascend the imposing ramparts of Craig Minnan, where a steep but surprisingly easy grassy rake leads to the summit and splendid views north to Ben Lomond and the Highland hills. Descend the same way to return to the stile at the fence junction. Cross and climb steadily up the grassy slopes of Windy Hil to reach the trig point, with more fine views across Glen Muirshiel to the heather moors beyond. Keep an eye out for moorland birds of prey such as hen harrier and peregrine hunting over the hillsides.

6 Return from here, omitting the climb up the two hills, to go over the ladderstile and on to the forest road and turn left. Continue on the steadily descending wide way until you reach a large turning area for forestry vehicles on the edge of the clear-fell. Turn right and take a narrow path that leads a few steps to the side of the conifers and then drops to the footbridge noted earlier – see point 3. Cross and climb the slope to join your outward path and go left. Press on until you can cross the next footbridge and walk down the other side of the burn, carrying on to the information board at the wall. Turn left and stride below the clear-fell to the waymark at the corner. Bear right to keep beside the larch and then the spruce, on the left, to reach the footbridge, which you cross.

7 Ignore your outward route and turn, right, up a delightful grassy path, through more deciduous tree plantings to a Y-junction. Turn right and follow the path as it winds left. Pass under the power lines and down through a gap onto the track taken earlier. Stroll right and follow the track as it winds right with the wall and trees to the right. Bear left with the track and as you near the outbuildings of Ward House, go right and in a few steps, left. This path takes you back to the track taken at the outset. Turn right and follow it back to the parking area.

Black Grouse

Practicals

Type of walk: *In good weather this is a very pleasant walk on paths and tracks, through mixed woodland, plantations, open areas and moorland. After heavy rain the ground might be too wet to progress to the two hills.*

Distance: 6 miles/9.5km
Time: 3–4 hours
Maps: OS Explorer 341/Landranger 63

Walk 35

Castle Semple

Park at Castle Semple Visitor Centre, Lochwinnoch, overlooking Castle Semple Loch, grid ref 357591. Access this by driving south-west along the A737 and leave it by the A760. Then turn north, following signs for Lochwinnoch village. Drive through the village, which is signed to the Visitor Centre and turn right along Saint Winnoc Road. The sign for the centre is beyond the turn.

Castle Semple Centre walk 35, Greenock Cut Centre walk 33 and Lunderston Bay walk 32, are all part of the **Clyde Muirshiel Regional Park**, whose headquarters are at Barnbrock. It is Scotland's largest Regional Park and is a protected landscape of over 280 sq km.

Collegiate Church, Castle Semple

The **Collegiate church**, now a picturesque ruin, was built in 1504 for John, first Lord Semple. A small college choir of resident clergy was asked to sing masses for the souls of his family in perpetuity. In 1513 Lord Sempill (the original spelling) was killed at the battle of Flodden. His tomb lies within the ruined church. The original Castle Semple, dating from the 1500s, was built on the lochside, where the farm now stands. It was demolished in the 18th century, and only the coach house now survives as part of privately owned farm buildings.

The Harvey family who later owned the Castle Semple estate, insisted that the two **railway bridges** were built in a sham castellated style. The Glasgow and South Western Railway Company had to accept these conditions before building the railway in the early 1900s .

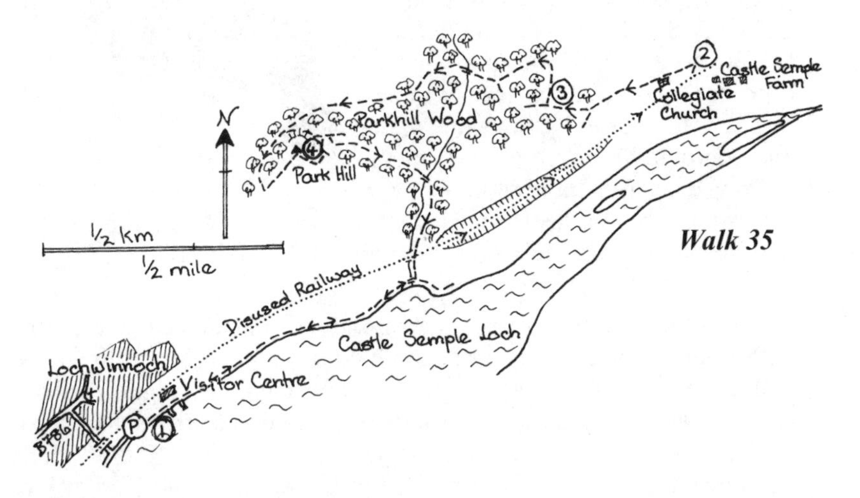

1 Walk along the good track beside the extensive Castle Semple Loch to your right, where you might spot goosanders fishing, a little group of goldeneye and lots of mute swans, including occasional whoopers. Follow the track to where it winds left. Before you ascend, look for the fine carving of otters on the trunk of a tree. There is also an interesting willow tunnel nearby. Then climb left and turn right to join the disused railway track now used by walkers and cyclists. Stride the tarmacked track, its sloping sides lined with trees, meadow sweet, wild roses and rosebay willow herb. As it passes through a cutting, the rock faces are adorned with a variety of ferns and mosses. In autumn, in the trees above, fieldfare and redwing, blackbird and thrush voraciously devour the lush crop of hawthorn berries. As you continue the wall to your right becomes much lower and you can see the loch again.

2 Just after viewing the ruined church through trees on the left, take a signed left turn dropping down through a gate. To the right stands one of the castellated bridges. Then turn left through another gate and climb to go through the small gate just above the ruin. Enjoy this delightful peaceful site, set among scattered trees and so well preserved by Historic Scotland. Go inside to see the ornate tomb and gravestones of other members of the Semple family. Then leave by the same gate and continue, left up the farm track. Follow it as it winds right to pass through a gate into deciduous Parkhill Wood. Walk on a short way to pass through a gateway and turn right off the main track as directed by a small yellow triangle on a post.

Wild roses

3 Descend the good path, cross a narrow stream and then climb a distinct path through rhododendrons as directed by another post with a small yellow triangle. Descend to a cross of paths and bear right, similarly waymarked. Climb steadily through woodland to come to the edge of the trees. Turn left and continue on, with good views, left, through the trees over the valley to the distant hills. Carry on along the high-level track, with fields to your right, and then descend gently until you reach a junction, where a track comes in on your left. Ignore this and press on ahead watching out for a lively bunch of tiny long tailed tits as you go. Carry on the track as it winds left, climbing steadily round the edge of Park Hill. Pause to look back to see several extensive lochs, stretching away to the skyline. At the brow you might wish to have your camera handy.

4 Descend the grassy trod from the brow and then wind round left into woodland and follow the lovely path, still high above the valley. As it goes down it curves. Join a wider path, turn right and almost immediately right again, as waymarked, to view a small stone grotto, with a small pool opposite. Then continue on the winding path through pleasing woodland sloping upwards on both sides. Go

over a footbridge and continue down, to the right, through a belt of woodland, with a pretty stream dancing through the trees on your right. Cross the railway track and descend the track you walked earlier. Wind right to return to the Visitor Centre on the lochside path.

Goldeneye

Practicals

Type of walk: *A splendid walk along the loch shore and through magnificent woodland. Lots of interest along the way.*

Distance: 4 miles/6.5km

Time: 2–3 hours

Maps: OS Explorer 341/Landranger 63

Walk 36

Gleniffer Braes Country Park, Renfrewshire

The Country Park Information Centre and car park lie to the south of Paisley, grid ref 482608. Access is by the B774. Turn right, south west, into Glenfield Road, cross the head of Thornley Dam, and a short way along look for two signboards for the centre, on the left, almost obscured by vegetation.

Waterfall, Gleniffer Braes

Gleniffer Braes Country Park is just over three miles long and one mile wide. It is situated on the edge of the **Clyde Plateau Lavas,** and from it there are wonderful views over the Lower Clyde Valley to Ben Lomond and the Arrochar Alps beyond. The park is mainly moorland, with forested areas, woodland and hill farming, and there are paths everywhere. The volcanic lavas provide soil rich in minerals and this is responsible for the diverse flora, with plants such as greater butterfly orchid and mountain pansy. These abound especially in areas grazed by cattle – Highland cattle here.

Walk 36

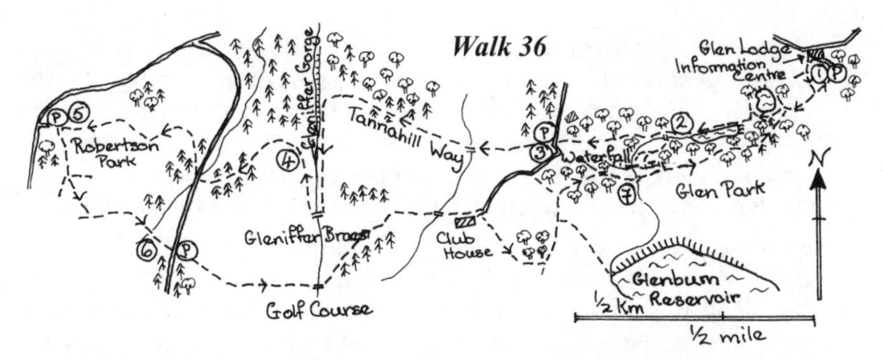

1 From the car park walk down the access track to the Visitor Centre. Turn left to walk up a signed track in the direction of Robertson Park and Tannahill. Wind round right on the metalled path. Turn right at a junction and, after a few steps, take an easily missed railed narrow path, left, that descends quite steeply through trees to a tiny lochan on your right. Go on to cross a metal footbridge, wind left to climb to a small reservoir and stroll on along its right side. It is almost surrounded by trees where fieldfares and redwings pause on the tops. On your left is a small stream hurrying down to join the pond. Where the track divides, take the left branch signposted 'To the waterfall'.

Mountain Pansy

2 Go down steps, cross the little stream and climb the other side, passing Tannahill Well as you go. Ignore the flight of steps on the left and go on along the narrow railed path round a bend to see a magnificent waterfall plummeting down a sheer wall of rock, covered with small water-loving plants. The fall hits projecting rocks as it goes and then drops in a single fall into a seething plunge pool before hurrying on towards the reservoir. Return to the junction and turn sharp left, ignoring the long flight of steps once more. Carry on and at the top of the slope, ignore the stile, and continue left through the pleasing woodland. Look left across the ravine to see the waterfall, just visited, through trees. Go on through a small clearing and ahead through gates to Braehead Road.

3 Cross, go through a car park and wind left with the track and out onto open moorland, to look down on Paisley's Stanely Reservoir and its ruined castle, the Highland hills and the end of the Campsies. Climb gently on the Tannahill Walkway, beside a pine forest, and then wind round left with the Gleniffer Burn deep in its gorge, cut along a geological fault, to your right. Go past the danger sign for the derelict bridge and keep beside the ravine to cross the burn higher up by a wooden bridge. Turn right and walk a wide grassy path down the opposite bank to reach the reinforced track you would have taken from the far side of the damaged bridge. You may see brown hares here.

4 Stride on left to continue over park-like pasture and then the way becomes needle strewn as the path passes between larch on one side and Scots pine on the other. Beyond, the track leads down to a metal gate onto Sergeant Law Road. Cross and take a gate opposite to bear right along a grassy trod and then between two belts of pines. Go slightly left over open ground to go through a gate. Bear left and then right on a reinforced track along the escarpment of the Clyde Plateau with more splendid views down to Paisley. There is a view indicator here just before the Robertson car park, where there are seats, picnic tables and swings. From here you can see the volcanic plug, Dumgoyne at the end of the Campsies. When the weather permits, you can also see Ben Lomond.

5 By the last log seat, walk, left, up towards and alongside woodland to go through a gate. Take the middle of three paths to walk south-east through a large area of rough ground, winding left and then right to join a track and reach the road crossed earlier. Go through the little car park and then a gate to carry on keeping parallel with a hedge and fence to your right, behind which is Paisley golf club. Look for mountain pansies in the short grazed grass. Carry on along the trod, which runs to the left of a large plantation. Well away to the left is another plantation. Follow the trod as it moves to the middle of the pasture between these two and then move slightly left to avoid a boggy area. Ahead to the far right is the golf clubhouse and its tall white flag pole. Make your way over indistinct paths towards these two.

6 Cross a small stream on a plank bridge and then go through a gate into the car park. Head left to another gate out of the parking area. Cross the pasture, half-right, to the top corner of beech woodland and carry on along its top-side on a tractor-marked way, with Glenburn Reservoir seen ahead in the distance. The heavily indented tractor wheel way winds steadily left and brings you to a gate. Here take the hedged, reinforced track beyond that leads pleasingly down to the end of a narrow lane where a branch goes off towards the reservoir. Cross and go on ahead along a continuing metalled track towards woodland. At the edge of this wood, where the track turns left, go down steps into trees and turn right to follow a good track through fine woodland.

7 At the T-junction, turn right to cross a plank bridge, just above a cascading burn, into an open area. Ignore the left turn to the splendid waterfall, seen earlier, and carry on the delightful high-level way, with a huge ravine to your left. Soon the trees begin to crowd in on the path. Press on, ignoring all left turns and turn right when you can see the ponds, left, walked beside earlier. Go on along the good track and at the open area curve right and then left. Descend towards the visitor centre and, after a short way, take a path on the right of the tarmacked track that leads straight down to the car park.

Brown Hare

Practicals

Type of walk: *Very satisfactory, a walk of delightful contrasts.*

Distance:	5 miles/8km
Time:	3 hours
Maps:	OS Explorer342/Landranger 64

Walk 37

Neilston Pad, Renfrewshire

Park at grid ref 472543. The small isolated car park lies at a sharp bend on an unclassified road, accessed by another unclassified road leading south from Neilston. The latter is accessed by a left turn off the A736, two miles west of Barrhead. Turn left in the centre of Neilston, and drive two miles from the village along a very straight road. Then take a left turn, marked by signs for a trout fishery.

Neilston, a dormitory for Glasgow, lies in the Levern Valley. There has been a church on the site of the present parish church since 1163.

Neilston Pad

Neilston Pad, overlooking Neilston, shows a craggy face on its eastern side. Its local geology is basalt.

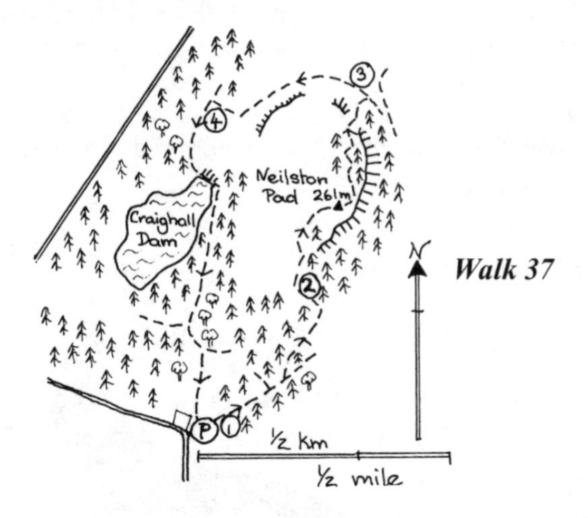

1 Take the farm gate out of the parking area to walk a wide reinforced track into a conifer plantation. Where a wide track comes in on the left, look for a narrow waymarked path, just beyond, on the left, climbing gently between the trees to open ground. Carry on ascending until just before a seat, where the way winds left, with a fine view down to Snypes Dam. Stroll on to cross a fence by a stile.

2 Climb steadily upwards, keeping parallel with the fence, passing widely scattered badly wind-blown Scots pine to reach the little summit marked with a small cairn, 853ft/260m. Then go on across a field of purple moor grass, still on a distinct path. The path winds left into more woodland and then descends a steep, rocky path that eases the gradient by twisting back and forth, tightly, over tree roots, stones and rocky steps on the edge of deciduous woodland. Take care as you drop down this pleasing way as it can be slippery.

3 At the foot, pause in this remote corner to look north-east to glimpse the outskirts of Glasgow. Then press on, left, on a good path, with the hill, now rearing upwards showing its steep grassy side, with lateral lines of soil slippage. There are crags at the top and a solitary tree close by. Here you might spot a kestrel quartering the slope. Climb a ladder-stile on the right and walk on into more forestry, climbing a steepish path into the trees.

4 On reaching a wide reinforced track, turn left to continue through more conifers and then when the trees cease you have a good view of the steep side of the hill once more. Continue on along the dam of Craighall Dam where you might spot goldeneye, coot and goosander. Wind on round on the track, now close under the hill with the loch to the right. Once past the lovely pool, ignore a signposted right turn and go on to wind round left with the good track. Here look for a way-marked path going off right through scrubby vegetation. This level narrow way leads you to a gap stile into the car park.

Goosander

Practicals

Type of walk: *Easy climb leading to a rare reward. Takes you through conifers and rough pasture to climb a delectable hill, returning under the hill, beside Craighall Dam.*

Distance: 2 ¼ miles/3.5km
Time: 1–2 hours
Maps: OS Explorer 333/Landranger 64

Walk 38

Calderwood Trail, Calderglen

Park in the main car park, well signposted off the A726, grid ref 654526. Access this from south of East Kilbride. It is signed all the way from Junction 5 on the M74 if you approach from the north.

This walk, the Calderwood Trail, winds downstream along the banks of the Rotten Calder (Rotten a corruption of a word meaning 'red' referring to the ironstone over which the burn flows) to the **Castle Falls**. There are more superb waterfalls to be seen along the way.

Castle Falls, Calderglen

By 1951 the castle had to be demolished. It stood at the end of the trail and was built in 1790 for the Maxwell family. When the lineage ended the castle, after a number of owners, was bought by the **Scottish Co-operative Society** who opened the grounds to the public in the early 20th century.

In 1979 it was designated a **Country Park** and opened officially in 1982. It was designed to allow the people of the new town of East Kilbride access to the countryside and was created from the estates of Torrance and Calderwood. The Visitor Centre and facilities are located in Torrance House, the oldest part of which was built in 1605.

1 From the parking area, keep right of the Conservatory, following signs for Nature Trails and Adventure Playground. Then take a footpath, left, between the fire pond and the playground, waymarked with a small red castle on a low post. At the T-junction turn right along a track to descend an easily-missed footpath, dropping left of the track, down to the river, through lofty trees. Go with the path as it winds left and passes into a Scots pine plantation. The path then ascends and turns right, high above the river. It soon descends steps to cross the Kingfisher footbridge where you might spot a kingfisher flying fast upstream. Here you might also spot a small group of long tailed tits, twittering, as they flit through the bushes close beside the bridge.

2 Walk on along the path, with a pasture to the right, to reach steps up to the road. At the top turn left over the narrow Newhousemill bridge, with care – the footpaths are narrow and the road is hardly wide enough for one car at a time. Cross at the end of the bridge and walk the footpath with the Rotten Calder to your right again. Soon high cliffs rise sheer on the opposite bank.

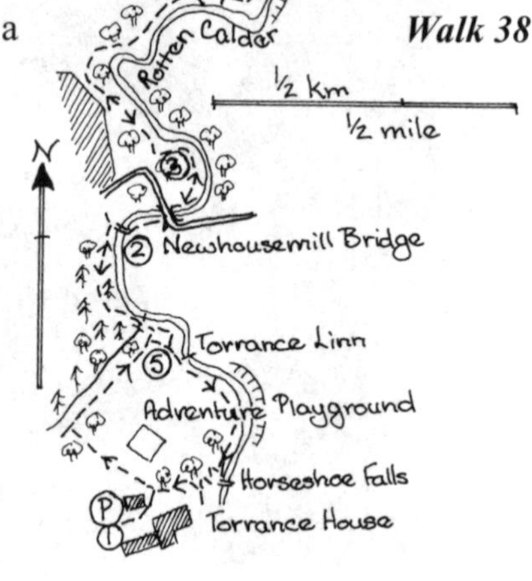

Walk 38

Scots pine

3 After 330yds/300m don't miss the path's unmarked sharp left turn up steps to the continuing way above the river. Go on the needle-strewn path with glimpses through the deciduous trees of the hurrying water far below. Climb more steps and walk right soon to pass a school on the left, then descend a sloping path below glorious beech and continue on, ignoring an anglers' path dropping right. Head on the very high-railed way, pass a seat and descend steps to a footbridge over a tributary. Beyond go on descending to come beside the lively burn. Follow a waymarked path, right, where the track divides, to see plummeting Trough Linn and press on along the fenced way beside the cascading river to rejoin the main track from where you can view Black Linn, another dramatic fall.

4 Follow the level way, with the Calder Gorge to the right and a narrower burn hurrying through its own steep-sided gorge to left. Soon, descend steadily to a footbridge. Beyond, turn left and begin to climb a long winding easy flight of steps to continue right along a high-level path. After 380yds/350m, descend again to a sign directing you to the site of the original castle. Go on here if you wish though there is little to see. This walk turns sharp right and descends a railed way along the side of the Calder to see the spectacular Castle Falls. Head on along the path and follow it up a slope to rejoin your outward route. From now on retrace your outward route to cross Newhousemill Bridge and then Kingfisher Bridge.

5 Just as you move into the coniferous woodland, turn left and descend to the side of the river once more. Walk upstream to admire the fine fall at Torrance Linn. Carry on to reach the superb Horseshoe Falls. After pausing here, turn right to take the sloping ramps and steps to return to the side of the Adventure playground and then the car park.

Grey squirrel

Practicals

Type of walk: *This is a glorious linear walk – there and back generally by the same route. Very good paths; exposed high level paths are railed but there are many mainly easy steps both up and down. A lovely time to do this walk is late October or early November when for all the way the trees are 'alight' with the yellows, golds and browns of autumn.*

Distance: 5 miles/8km
Time: 3 ½ hours
Maps: OS Explorer 334/Landranger 64

Walk 39

Chatelherault and the Avon Gorge

Park in the very large parking area at Chatelherault Country Park, grid ref 738538. Access this by the M74 and then take the A72 at Junction 7 towards Hamilton. The entrance to the country park is in the village of Ferniegair, 1 ½ miles/2.5km south east of Hamilton. The park is signed from the M74.

The **country park** is centred on the former hunting lodge of the now demolished Hamilton Palace. The lodge was designed by William Adam and completed in 1734. It provided kennels, stables and accommodation for hunting parties. An avenue of lime trees linked the lodge with the palace.

Chatelherault Country Park takes its name from the French town of the same name, the title Duc de Chatelherault being held by the Duke of Hamilton. The lodge was a gift from the French king to the

Chatelherault

2nd Duke of Arran, a Hamilton. It was an expensive folly built in the mid-18th century to give an impression of grandeur.

Cadzow Castle when in use was known as the Castle in the Wood of Hamilton. From its architectural details it is believed to date from between 1500 and 1550. It was demolished in 1928. The ruins, glowing a rosy pink in the sunshine, stand on a small grassy hill, surrounded by trees.

1 Walk from the car park towards the Visitor Centre and, just before the entrance, stand and peruse the information board and the large map. Then walk left to take the first right and follow the signs for 'all other routes'. Pass under lofty mixed conifers on a curving path to cross Duke's Bridge over the immensely deep wooded gorge through which flows the Avon Water. Beyond, after a few steps, wind right to climb a short way to see the picturesque ruins of Cadzow Castle which, alas, might be surrounded by scaffolding.

2 Turn acute left and follow a grassy track to rejoin, at the top of a slope, the track from the bridge. Continue, right, on the track as it winds a little left, and then right, along the ridge, high above the steep-sided, densely tree-clad Avon gorge to pass an information board, on the right, for Cadzow Oaks and Earthworks, which you might wish to visit. From the continuing path you have a wonderful view of the magnificent oaks, some more than 200 years old. Carry on the winding way, with fields to the right and then on through Divoty Glen, with a hay meadow to the right and masses of rosebay willow herb and meadowsweet, colourful and sweet-scented, beside the path.

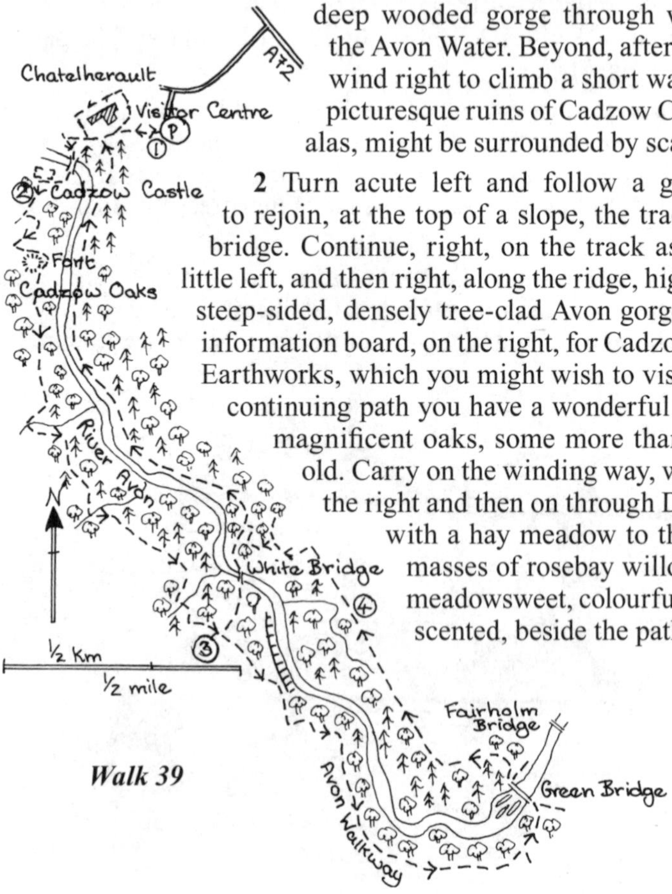

Walk 39

3 Ignore the path that drops down to White Bridge. Keep ahead on the path with more agricultural land to the right. To the left dense forest drops so steeply that there is no view of the gorge or the Avon at all. Head on the good path as it eventually curves left through the forest and descends to the very long Green Bridge, which crosses mire at first and then the wide Avon Water. Beyond, go ahead and begin your ascent of the well constructed, easy, but so many, steps up to the ridge on the opposite side of the gorge.

4 Walk on the pleasing way. Pass through an open area below the power lines crossing the gorge and, a short way along, turn left to descend a signposted long row of steps in the direction of White Bridge. At the foot of this row of steps, bear right on a track to descend more steps to see the river through trees, surging and peat stained. Continue on the wide easy-to-walk track, enjoying the Avon Water, where you may see dippers and grey wagtails. At the Y-junction take the upper path, climbing steadily through conifers, high above the river, to return to the Visitor Centre.

Grey Wagtail

Practicals

Type of walk: *A fine forest walk with very good paths all the way. The last section beside the Avon Water is a delight. Though there are many steps up from the Green Bridge and many more to descend towards the river near the White Bridge, they are well graded and well constructed and vital after heavy rain.*

Distance: 5 miles/8km
Time: 3 hours
Maps: OS Explorer 343/Landranger 64

Walk 40

Baron's Haugh and Dalzell Park, Motherwell

Park in the large RSPB car park, grid ref 756552, on the right of the road leading into the reserve. To reach this leave the M74 at Junction 6, turning east for Motherwell on the A723. Take the first turn on the right, B754, after crossing the Clyde. Go over the railway above Airbles Station, and turn right at the next roundabout. Turn right at the next T-junction, then left and immediately right at the next main junction. Bear left at a fork, into the reserve. The car park is on the right.

The High Arch Bridge, Dalzell

Baron's Haugh is an RSPB reserve on the edge of the Clyde below Motherwell. It is mainly marshland with wide shallow pools and some wet meadows. The RSPB can control the water levels to suit the birds. The reserve is also grazed by cattle. In winter it hosts a wide variety of duck such as wigeon, teal, mallard, pochard and tufted duck and a large 'herd' of whooper swans. In spring and autumn, look for waders such as greenshanks, snipe, ruff, common sandpiper. Kingfishers and goosander occur on the Clyde nearby all year round.

Dalzell House was lived in by the Hamiltons, from the 17th century until the early 1950s. It is still private but the estate is now open to the public. There are many paths and the whole estate is laid out like a large garden, with decorative bridges, a gazebo and a Japanese garden.

1 Return out of the car park and turn right, downhill. About 22yds/20m further on go through a kissing gate beside a gate on the right and carry on down a surfaced way through mature woodland. The path winds right at the foot of the slope. Take the first path on the left, through reeds, purple loosestrife and hairy willow herb. This leads down to the Marsh Hide, where you might spot greenshank, heron and lapwings at the right time of year.

Snipe

2 Return to the main path and turn left to carry on in the previous direction. Ignore a path on the right. The path now runs along with woodland to the left and fields on the right. The next hide, Causeway Hide, is soon reached on the left. Here look for snipe, dabchick, black-headed

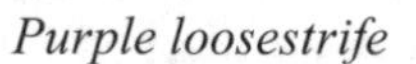

Purple loosestrife

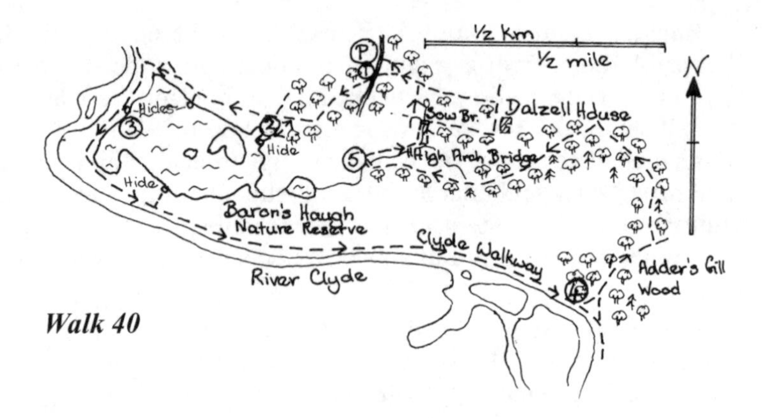

Walk 40

gull, cormorant and duck in winter. Return to the path. At the next junction take the left, waymarked, branch, which continues along an embankment through woodland to reach the River Clyde. Turn left on the tarmacked path, which is part of the Clyde Walkway. The river is wide and slow-flowing here, flanked with willows. Here you might see goosander and possibly kingfisher. The path is bordered with Himalayan balsam.

3 Visit Phoenix Hide on the left, then continue on the walkway. Some distance beyond the next corner is Centenary Hide. Stroll the paved way, with only occasional glimpses of the river through the vegetation in summer, until eventually you reach a bridge over a tributary burn, and a gate. Go through and walk on beside the now visible river, with mature lime trees on both sides of the path.

4 Take the waymarked path on the left, which leaves the Clyde Walkway just before the next gate and head uphill into the trees through a small valley, Adder's Gill. Head on uphill, joining a path from the right, and continue climbing until you come to a signed junction. Take the left branch and walk on through the lovely mature woodland, mainly deciduous but with, in places, a dense understorey of yew. When you reach a Y-junction go left downhill. Ignore two right turns and carry on until, eventually, you descend steps to cross a bridge over the Dalzell Burn.

5 Turn right and walk up past a mausoleum, then St. Patrick's Well and Lord Gavin's Gazebo. The path keeps close to the burn and is fenced as it rises above the water. Pass a low arched bridge then, further up the glen, you reach the High Arch Bridge. You cannot cross because the structure is dangerous, but it is very delicate and beautiful. Just beyond there is a fork in the path and if you go right you can get a better view of the bridge. Carry on up a flight of steps to cross a side gully below Sow Bridge, an imposing and substantial structure, which carries the main drive over to Dalzell House. At the far side of the bridge climb steps to turn right along a track at the top. Cross the main carriage drive and ascend a tree lined walk. To your right is the Japanese Garden, with a pool. At the next cross of paths turn left. Then take the next right turn to return to the car park.

Greenshank

Practicals

Type of walk: *Very pleasant, along good tracks and paths, sometimes surfaced. The views of the river are fine but possibly even better in winter when the vegetation has died down. The bird-watching is excellent, especially in winter and at migration times (May, August and September).*

Distance: 3½ miles/5.5km
Time: 2–3 hours
Maps: OS Explorer 343/Landranger 64

Walking Scotland Series
from Clan Books

MARY WELSH AND CHRISTINE ISHERWOOD have completed this series of guides covering the whole of Scotland's mainland and principal islands.

Full list of volumes available:

1. WALKING THE ISLE OF ARRAN
2. WALKING THE ISLE OF SKYE
3. WALKING WESTER ROSS
4. WALKING PERTHSHIRE
5. WALKING THE WESTERN ISLES
6. WALKING ORKNEY
7. WALKING SHETLAND
8. WALKING THE ISLES OF ISLAY, JURA AND COLONSAY
9. WALKING GLENFINNAN: THE ROAD TO THE ISLES
10. WALKING THE ISLES OF MULL, IONA, COLL AND TIREE
11. WALKING DUMFRIES AND GALLOWAY
12. WALKING ARGYLL AND BUTE
13. WALKING DEESIDE, DONSIDE AND ANGUS
14. WALKING THE TROSSACHS, LOCH LOMONDSIDE AND THE CAMPSIE FELLS
15. WALKING GLENCOE, LOCHABER AND THE GREAT GLEN
16. WALKING STRATHSPEY, MORAY, BANFF AND BUCHAN
17. WALKING AROUND LOCH NESS, THE BLACK ISLE AND EASTER ROSS
18. WALKING CAITHNESS AND SUTHERLAND
19. WALKING THE SCOTTISH BORDERS AND EAST LOTHIAN
20. WALKING AYRSHIRE, RENFREWSHIRE AND LANARKSHIRE
21. WALKING FIFE, THE OCHILS, TAYSIDE AND THE FORTH VALLEY